The Early Church Today Series

ABBA AMMONAS

THE LETTERS OF ABBA AMMONAS

THE EARLY CHURCH TODAY SERIES

Volume 4

The early leaders of the Church, tasked with shepherding Christ's flock, left us spiritual wealth that is too often neglected in modern times. The Early Church Today Series, published by the St. Mary & St. Moses Abbey Press, aims to help make that richness more accessible to readers, inviting them to see the applicability of the early Church to our walk with God today. By sharing practical selections from the writings of the early Church, aided by meaningful editorial supplements and revisions, each book will attempt to diminish impediments and bring to light what the Church has to offer.

The Letters of Abba Ammonas

The Disciple and Successor of
St. Anthony the Great

Translated with an Introduction by
St. Mary and St. Moses Abbey

The Letters of Abba Ammonas

Copyright © 2024 Coptic Orthodox Diocese of the Southern U.S.A.

All rights reserved.

Designed & Published by:
St. Mary & St. Moses Abbey Press
101 S Vista Dr, Sandia, TX 78383
stmabbeypress.com

Translation from Arabic by St. Mary & St. Moses Abbey.

All Scripture quotations in the footnotes of this book, unless otherwise indicated, are taken from the New King James Version® Copyright © 1982 by Thomas Nelson, Inc. Used by permission. All rights reserved.

Cover Icon: Wall icon of Abba Ammoes and Abba John the Short, housed in St. Mary and St. Moses Abbey. The icon portrays the story of the tree of obedience, wherein Abba Ammoes gave a dry stick to his disciple Abba John and asked him to water it every day until it bore fruit.

CONTENTS

Introduction	7
The First Letter	19
The Second Letter	25
The Third Letter	28
The Fourth Letter	33
The Fifth Letter	37
The Sixth Letter	41
The Seventh Letter	45
The Eighth Letter	50
The Ninth Letter	54
The Tenth Letter	72
The Eleventh Letter	92
The Twelfth Letter	102
The Thirteenth Letter	112

INTRODUCTION

Who is Abba Ammonas?

Abba Ammonas[1] was a disciple of St. Anthony the Great, and after the departure of St. Anthony, he succeeded him in directing the brethren living in the Outer Mountain of Pispir.[2] Biographical information about him is exceedingly scarce, and what is known is gleaned primarily from the *Apophthegmata Patrum*[3] and *Historia Monachorum in Aegypto*[4]; nevertheless, from the little that is known, Abba Ammonas emerges as one of the greatest desert

---

1   His name is spelled in a number of ways. For consistency, we maintain the spelling "Ammonas" throughout the text, as it appears in the English translation from Greek.
2   See D.J. Chitty *The Desert a City*. (Crestwood, NY: SVS Press, 1995), 38. The Lives of the Desert Fathers, N. Russell, trans. (Oxford, UK: Mowbray, 1981), 99.
3   For English translation from Greek see: *Give Me a Word: The Alphabetical Sayings of the Desert Fathers*, J. Wortley, trans. (Yonkers, NY: SVS Press, 2014).
4   For English translation from Greek see: *The Lives of the Desert Fathers*, N. Russell, trans. (Oxford, UK: Mowbray, 1981).

personalities of the fourth century AD.

Abba Ammonas was discipled unto St. Anthony and knew what the latter did in secret. This is made manifest from the following story:

> Some brothers visited Abba Antony and repeated to him a verse from Leviticus. The elder went out into the desert and, without his knowing, Abba Ammonas followed him, for he was aware of his habits. When he had gone a very long way, standing to pray, the elder called out in a loud voice: "O God, send Moses and he will teach me [the meaning of] this verse"—and there came a voice speaking with him. Abba Ammonas said: "I heard the voice speaking with him but did not comprehend the meaning of what was said."[5]

St. Anthony himself prophesied that Abba Ammonas would become great. And though he was ordained as a bishop[6], Abba Ammonas maintained such a profound degree of humility, that he would not cast judgment on sinners, but rather behaved in a peculiar—and even seemingly unseemly—manner. The following was said concerning him:

> On one occasion Abba Ammonas went to

---
5 *Give Me a Word: The Alphabetical Sayings of the Desert Fathers*, J. Wortley, trans. (Yonkers, NY: SVS Press, 2014), Anthony 26.
6 See Alphabetical Sayings, Ammonas 8 and 10.

Abba Anthony, and he lost the way, and sat down for a little and fell asleep; and he rose up from his slumber, and prayed unto God, and said, "I beseech You, O Lord God, not to destroy that which You have fashioned." Then he lifted up his eyes, and, behold, there was the form of a man's hand above him in the heavens, and it showed him the way until he came and stood above the cave of Abba Anthony; and when he had gone into the cave to the old man, Abba Anthony prophesied unto him, saying, "You shall increase in the fear of God." Then he took him outside the cave, and showing him a stone, said, "Curse this stone, and smite it," and he did so, and Abba Anthony said unto him, "It is thus that you shall arrive at this state, for you shall bear heaviness, and great abuse;" and this actually happened to Abba Ammonas. Now, through his abundant goodness Abba Ammonas knew not wickedness. And after he had become a Bishop, through his spiritual excellence they brought unto him a virgin who had conceived, and they said unto him, "So-and-so has done this deed; let them receive correction;" but he made the sign of the Cross over her belly, and ordered them to give her six pairs of linen cloths, and he said, "Peradventure when she brings forth either she or the child will die, [and if either dies] let them be buried." Then those who were with him said unto him, "What is this that you have done? Give the command that they receive correction." And he said unto them, "See, O my brethren, she is near unto death, and what can I do?" Then he dismissed her. And the old man never ventured to judge anyone, for he was full of lovingkindness and endless goodness to all the children of men.[7]

A similar incident was also related concerning him not passing judgment:

They used to say of him that some folk came to be judged before him but the elder feigned insanity. Here there was a woman standing near to him and she was saying to her neighbor: "This elder is mad." The elder heard her; he called out to her and said: "How I labored away in the desert in order to acquire this madness and, because of you, I am going to lose it today!"[8]

In the aforementioned story, Abba Ammonas

---

[7] *The Paradise of the Holy Fathers* 2, A.W. Budge, trans. (London, UK: Chatto & Windus, 1907), 106. Cf. Alphabetical Sayings, Ammonas 7 and 8.

[8] *Give Me a Word: The Alphabetical Sayings of the Desert Fathers*, Wortley J., trans. (Yonkers, NY: SVS Press, 2014), Ammonas 9.

was perhaps speaking of the time he spent in Scetis, as he himself said:

> Abba Ammonas used to say, "I have spent fourteen years in Scetis in making supplication unto God by day and by night that He would grant me to overcome anger."[9]

It seems that Abba Ammonas consciously pursued this manner of life and course of action, not out of fear or weakness, but out of love. For his heart abounded with love for all. The following story may help illustrate this point:

> On one occasion Abba Ammonas came to a certain place to eat with the brethren, and there was there a brother concerning whom evil reports were abroad, for it had happened that a woman had come and entered his cell. And when all the people who were living in that place heard [of this], they were troubled, and they gathered together to expel that brother from his cell, and learning that the blessed Bishop Ammonas was there, they came and entreated him to go with them. Now when the brother knew [this], he took the woman and hid her under an earthenware vessel. And much people having assembled, and Abba Ammonas, understanding what

---

9 *The Paradise of the Holy Fathers* 2, A.W. Budge, trans. (London, UK: Chatto & Windus, 1907), 210. Cf. Alphabetical Sayings, Ammonas 3.

that brother had done, for the sake of God hid the matter. And he went in and sat upon the earthenware vessel, and commanded that the cell of the brother should be searched, but although they examined the place they found no one there. Then Abba Ammonas answered and said, "What is this that you have done? May God forgive you;" and he prayed and said, "Let all the people go forth," and finally he took the brother by the hand, and said unto him, "Take heed to your soul, O my brother," and having said this he departed, and he refused to make public the matter of the brother.[10]

The following was also related of him, showing his discipline and wisdom:

Abba Ammonas once came to cross the river and, finding the ferry ready to go, he sat himself down. Then here there came another boat to that place and took on the people who were there. They said to him: "You come too, abba; cross with us," but he said: "I only go on board the public ferry." He had a sheaf of palm-fronds [with him]; he sat there braiding a rope and undoing it again until they made the crossing—that was how he crossed over. The brothers prostrated themselves, saying: "Why did you do that?"

---

10 Ibid., 92. Cf. Alphabetical Sayings, Ammonas 10.

And the elder said to them: "So that I am not always going around with my thought[11] engaged." But this too is an indication of how we should travel the way of God in a calm state of mind.[12]

Several supernatural and miraculous occurrences were recounted concerning Abba Ammonas, revealing his humility, boldness of his prayers, and his gift of clairvoyance. The story when Abba Ammonas was lost on his way to St. Anthony shows that because of his humility, God worked the previously mentioned miracle with him. For though he was in danger of losing his life, Abba Ammonas did not deem himself worthy of asking God to be delivered miraculously, as one saint commented on this story.[13] It is also related concerning Abba Ammonas that he once saw a basilisk, as he went to draw water, and he prayed to God, and immediately it burst asunder through the power of God.[14] This story reveals the boldness of Abba Ammonas' prayers. The following story shows that he possessed the gift of clairvoyance, which is related as follows:

On one occasion tribulation came upon the

---

11 Gr. *logismos*.
12 *Give Me a Word: The Alphabetical Sayings of the Desert Fathers*, J. Wortley, trans. (Yonkers, NY: SVS Press, 2014), Ammonas 6.
13 See *The Ascetical Homilies of Saint Isaac the Syrian*. (Boston, MA: Holy Transfiguration Monastery, 2011), 432.
14 See *Give Me a Word: The Alphabetical Sayings of the Desert Fathers*, J. Wortley, trans. (Yonkers, NY: SVS Press, 2014), Ammonas 2.

monks in a certain place where they were living, and they wished to forsake it and come to Abba Ammonas; and behold, he was travelling in a boat, and he saw them going along by the side of the river, and he ordered the boatmen to bring [the boat] close to land. Then he called these brethren and said unto them, "I am Ammonas to whom you wish to go;" and he entreated them to go back to their place, and he comforted them, and told them to endure patiently, for there was in the matter no loss to the soul, but only human vexation.[15]

Abba Ammonas was sought after for guidance by monks, as an Abba possessing the gift of discernment, as the aforementioned story illustrated. Abba Poemen himself sought the guidance of Abba Ammonas when he was troubled regarding his brother's behavior. The story is recounted as follows:

> Paesius, the brother of Abba Poemen, had an affection for the people who were outside his monastery, and Abba Poemen did not wish this to be, and he rose up and fled to Abba Ammonas, and said unto him, "My brother Paesius has made a promise of love to certain folk, and I am not pleased thereat." Abba

---

15 *The Paradise of the Holy Fathers* 2, A.W. Budge, trans. (London, UK: Chatto & Windus, 1907), 232. Cf. Alphabetical Sayings, Ammonas 5.

Ammonas said unto him, "Poemen, you are still alive. Go, and sit in your cell, and meditate in your mind, saying, 'Behold, there is a year for you in the grave.'"[16]

Likewise the following two stories illustrate that monks travelled considerable distances, with much toil, to hear a word full of discernment from Abba Ammonas:

> One of the fathers used to relate that he had an old man in a cell[17], who performed many ascetic labors, and who clothed himself in a palm-leaf mat; and this old man went to Abba Ammonas, who, seeing that he wore a palm-leaf mat only, said unto him, "This will profit you nothing." And the old man asked him, saying, "Three thoughts vex me. Shall I go to the desert, or shall I go forth into exile, or shall I shut myself up in a cell, and receive no man, and eat once every two days?" Abba Ammonas said unto him, "You are not able to do any one of these things, but go, sit in your cell, and eat a very little food each day, and let there be in your heart always the words of the publican, 'God be merciful to me a sinner,' and thus you shall be able to live."[18]

---

16 Ibid., 52. Cf. Alphabetical Sayings, Poemen 2.
17 Alphabetical Sayings reads "at the Cells."
18 *The Paradise of the Holy Fathers* 2, A.W. Budge, trans. (London,

A brother asked Abba Ammonas: "Tell me a saying." The elder said: "Go and frame your thought[19] the way the evil-doers who are in prison do, for they are always asking people: 'Where is the governor and when is he coming?'—weeping in expectation. So ought the monk always to pay heed and to be reproaching his own soul, saying: 'Ah me! How can I stand before the judgment seat of Christ and how can I defend myself before him?' If you deliberate like this all the time, you can be saved."[20]

The greatness of his discernment is also made manifest in the following words he gave:

An old man was asked, "What is the straight and narrow way?" And he answered and said, "The straight and narrow way is for a man to constrain his thoughts, and to restrain his desires for God's sake, and this [is intended to be understood when] it is said, 'Behold, we have left everything and followed You.'"[21]

UK: Chatto & Windus, 1907), 105. Cf. Alphabetical Sayings, Ammonas 4.

19 Gr. *logismos*.

20 *Give Me a Word: The Alphabetical Sayings of the Desert Fathers*, J. Wortley, trans. (Yonkers, NY: SVS Press, 2014), Ammonas 1.

21 *The Paradise of the Holy Fathers* 2, A.W. Budge, trans. (London, UK: Chatto & Windus, 1907), 198. Cf. Alphabetical Sayings, Ammonas 11.

Abba Poemen used to say that Abba Ammonas said, "One man spends the whole period of his life holding an axe in his hand [ready] to cut down a tree, and never finds the opportunity of wielding it; and another man, who knows well how to fell trees, hews with three [strokes of the] axe, and wields them [against trees]." He said, "Now, the axe [in this case] is discretion [or discernment]."[22]

Abba Ammonas said, "A man may pass one hundred years in his cell, and not know rightly how a monk should live in his cell, or even how to live secluded for one day." And he used to say, "The proper way and manner for a monk to live is to condemn himself continually."[23]

The Letters

Thirteen letters are attributed to Abba Ammonas. In Arabic, they appear as part of the collection of the letters of St. Anthony the Great, which consists of twenty letters. The first seven letters were authored by St. Anthony himself.[24] The remaining

---

22 Ibid., 183. Cf. Alphabetical Sayings, Poemen 52.
23 Ibid., 116. Cf. Alphabetical Sayings, Poemen 95.
24 See *The Letters of St. Anthony the Great*. (Sandia, TX: St. Mary & St. Moses Abbey Press, 2023).

thirteen letters were authored by Abba Ammonas, the disciple of St. Anthony, translated into English in this book.

The Arabic text was taken from *Bostan Al-Rohban Al-Mowasah, Al-joz' Al-Awal* [The Expanded Paradise of the Monks, Volume 1]. (Egypt: St. Macarius Monastery, 2006), henceforth *Expanded Paradise*; and *Rawdat Al-Nofous Fi Rasa'il Al-Kidees Antonious* [The Paradise of the Souls in the Letters of Saint Anthony]. (Egypt: St. Anthony Monastery, 1899), henceforth *The Paradise of the Souls*. Both books were used for this translation, though we relied mainly on the former, to obtain a more accurate English translation. The collector of the material of the latter book, the monk Andrawis of St. Anthony Monastery, Egypt, indicates that the text was taken from the oldest copy that was previously translated from Coptic.

THE FIRST LETTER

To his children, the monks, urging them to struggle, to receive the fiery Holy Spirit here [on earth], so they gather there [in heaven]. And he reminds them of his struggles, and informs them of what had happened to him, to motivate them. This letter is read on the day of his departure.

1. Beloved in the Lord, I write to you as children beloved of their fathers. For the children according to the flesh, if they consider[25] their fathers and agree with them, the fathers love them with all their hearts, and honor them to the utmost, more than their children who are not obedient to them. And if they obtain something good, they lay it up for their children who agree with them and who imitate them. So if bodily fathers do so, how much more do our spiritual fathers want to give honors to their

---

25   Or: meditate upon.

children who agree with them and imitate them.

As for you, my beloved in the Lord, whom I love with all my heart, I desire to be always with you, and see you, and bless you. For your entering into a covenant with me, imitating me, and your return to God—all these I see to be upright; and you have taken abode in my heart for every reason. And now I beseech my God for your sakes, night and day, that He may give you His gifts, which He gave me by His grace only, not for [any] worthiness in me. For this is the great wealth which our Lord has given me, and I ask Him that He may give it to you too. And this is my utmost desire and my prayer always, night and day, that you may be with me in that place in which I will be when I depart from this body, because our Lord always hears me, from the time when I was little to this day, and I know that, in His mercy, He will hear me in this [matter] too.

2. I have written this to you, my children, for the sake of the greatness of the love of my heart for you, for through your struggle in the Lord, you have become like me in everything. And know that our Lord Christ, out of His great love, did so with His disciples, when He said to them, "I no longer call you servants, but brethren, loved ones, and sons."[26] And when they became sons to Him, He prayed the Father for their sakes, saying, "Father, I desire that these may be where I am, for I am in You, and they in

---

26 Cf. John 15:15.

Me, that all of us may be made perfect in oneness."[27] Therefore, look and understand, how our Lord Jesus besought the Father for His disciples, when they became sons to Him, that they may be with Him where He is. And so now, too, is my prayer, my loved ones, that we all may be in the place in which there is no sorrow, sickness, darkness, nor malicious spirits, but is filled with all gladness, light, eternal life, and the crowns that do not fade away, and other things are there, which the human tongue cannot describe, for they endure forever.

3. My children, pray to the Lord that He may facilitate my way to you once again, and that I may stay with you for some time. For I know that this is for your edification and your joy in the faith. And I too will rejoice if I come to you, that you may rejoice and grow all the more in the faith, and that I may make known to you many other mysteries which I cannot write to you in this letter. And your mother Sarah, who is the spirit, rejoices in you, she who has completed [the time of] her pregnancy and has given birth to a godly[28] spirit in you, and she longs to make you perfect, as I have asked her on your behalf, through that fiery, great Spirit, whom I have received, that you may receive Him too. And if you want to receive Him and have Him dwell in you, first offer the toils of the body and the humility of the heart, and lift up your thoughts to heaven night

---

27 Cf. John 17:21–24.
28 Or: divine.

and day, and ask with uprightness of heart for this fiery Spirit, and then He is given you, for this is how Elijah the Tishbite, Elisha, and all the prophets acquired Him.

Do not think in your hearts and be double-hearted. And do not say, "Who could accept this?" No, my children, do not let these thoughts come into your hearts; rather, ask with uprightness of heart, and you will receive Him. And I too, your father, strive with you and pray for your sakes, that you may receive Him, for I know that you are perfect and able to receive Him. For whoever cultivates himself in this husbandry, then the Spirit is given to him in every generation and forever. But I know that [some] people had received Him, and when they had failed to complete this husbandry, He did not abide in them.

4. As for you, my loved ones, whom I long to see, because of the uprightness of your minds, persist in praying diligently, with all your hearts, so He will be given to you, for the Spirit dwells in the upright hearts. And if you received Him, He would reveal to you the heavenly[29] mysteries and other things I cannot express on paper, with pen and ink. And He would take away from you the fear of men, of beasts, of desolate deserts, and all the like. And you would have heavenly joy, night and day, and you would be, [while] in this body, as those who are in

---

29 Literally: on high.

The First Letter

the Kingdom.

And then you should not pray for yourselves alone, but for others too, for whoever has received the Spirit should not pray only for himself, but also for others, as Moses the prophet did when he received the Spirit. He prayed for the people, saying to God, "If You destroy these, blot out my name from the book of life."[30] And likewise will the prayer be of all who reach this measure, of the saints and others, for I cannot describe them by name, one by one. As for you, you are wise and know them. As for me, my prayer now, night and day, is that you may have in you the greatness of the delight of the Spirit, whom all the pure have received.

5. My beloved children, after I had written this letter, the Spirit of God moved me[31] to write to you about the fiery Spirit at its end, and about divine love. And if I come to you, by the Lord's help, I will make known to you many other things about the Spirit, that you may acquire them all.

As I offered you peace in the beginning of this letter, so also I offer you peace, in the love of the Lord, in its end, in the fiery Spirit, whom I and you have received through the grace of the Lord. And I beseech you to abandon your sensual will, and to hold on to stillness of every kind, that the powers on high may dwell with you through the support of

---

30 Cf. Exodus 32:32.
31 *The Paradise of the Souls*: the Spirit of God moved in me.

the Holy Spirit, and help you to do the will of the Holy Trinity, Father and Son and Holy Spirit, to whom praise is [due] always, eternally, for ever and ever. Amen.

THE SECOND LETTER

To his children, the monks, informing them of the magnitude of the work of God's power in the saints, and urging them to acquire it, that they may receive the everlasting Kingdom

1. Beloved in the Lord, if a man loves God with all the heart, with all the mind, with all the intent, and with all the strength, he acquires the fear of God; and the fear begets weeping, and weeping begets power, and through the perfection of this in the soul, she [the soul] brings forth fruit in all things. And if the Lord sees these good fruits in the soul, He receives her[32] as an elect aroma of incense, and rejoices in her with the pure angels at all times, and gives her gladness and preserves her in all her ways, that she may reach her place of rest. And the devil does not prevail against her, for he sees the guardian from on high surrounding her, so he is afraid of approaching

---

32 I.e. the soul.

that person altogether because of that great power.

Now, my beloved in the Lord, whom my soul loves and knows that they love God, acquire this power for yourselves, that the devils may become afraid of you, and [that] the labors which you perform may become light, and [that] the divine [things] may become sweet to you, for the sweetness of the love of God is sweeter than honey in the comb. For many of the monks and nuns, who are [living] in communities, while they have not [actually] tasted the sweetness of the love of God and have not acquired the divine power, they thought they had acquired it, yet they have not received it because they have not traded in it, and therefore, God has not given it to them. So each [one] who has traded in it will receive it as a gift of God to him, for with God there is no partiality and He does not regard the person of men, but He in all generations, generation after generation, gives it to whoever does its works.

2. Now, my beloved in Christ, I know that you love God, so take heed that this be with all your hearts. And by this my heart rejoices, that you may be able to acquire the power of God, and may pass the rest of your lives in gladness and joy, and [that] the works of the Lord may become light upon you. For the power which is given to a man is what leads him to the places of rest and preserves him till he has passed through all the powers of the air. As the Psalm said, "Blessed is the man who shall fulfill his desire with them; they shall not be ashamed, when

The Second Letter

they speak to their enemies at the gate."[33]

Know then, my children, that as long as the light of God and His power are with a man, he despises the reproaches of the people of the world and their honors too. He also hates all that is in the world and the comforts of the body, and he cleanses his heart from evil thoughts, and thereupon he offers a fast and tears, night and day, with pure prayers, so our Lord gives him that same power.

Therefore, my blessed children, be diligent to acquire that power with which you would fulfill all your works with ease and lightness and would find a great boldness before the Lord, and He would fulfill to you all your prayers. And know that I had wanted to write to you many words because of my love for you, but I have limited it to these few [words], and I ask that our Lord Jesus Christ may make them for you a salvation and joy, to whom is due praise and honor, by all rational [beings], with His good Father and His Holy Spirit, forever and ever. Amen.

---

[33] Psalms 126:5 LXX, Orthodox Study Bible (OSB).

THE THIRD LETTER

To his children, the monks: on vainglory and its battles, and he informs them how they ought to struggle to be saved from it

1. My blessed children, I write to you this letter that you may know that those who love God and seek Him with all their hearts, He hears them and gives them all that they ask for. But those who do not come to Him with all their hearts, who are rather double-hearted, and all that they do apparently is rather to receive glory from men—those, God does not hear in anything they ask for, but He is angry with them all the more, because their works are [done] with hypocrisy. Therefore, the saying of the Psalm is fulfilled in them, "For God scattered the bones of men-pleasers."[34] For God—glory be to His mention—is angry with their works and is not pleased with their prayers, but He opposes

---
34   Psalms 52:6 LXX, OSB.

The Third Letter

them all the more, because they complete their works unfaithfully, doing them to please[35] men. And therefore, the power of God is not working in them, because they are fainthearted in all the works they begin. Therefore, they have not known the divine sweetness, nor its lightness, nor its joy, but their works have become burdensome upon their souls, as is a heavy burden. Many of their kind[36] are likewise. This malicious spirit deceived them and made them fulfill their works to please[37] men, because they have not acquired this power which gives delight to the soul, and fills it with joy and gladness day by day, and kindles in it a divine fire.

2. But you, my beloved, beloved of my heart, who have offered the fruits of your toils before the Lord, be diligent to keep far from the spirit of vainglory, and to always prevail against it, that our Lord may accept your fruits which you offer before Him and [that] you may receive from Him the power which is given to His elect. My heart is comforted because of you, my beloved, for I know that you do not consent to the spirit of vainglory, but oppose it at all times; and therefore, your fruit is pure and living. Therefore, continue in opposing that evil spirit, for when a person starts with righteous works and good diligence, this spirit comes to him, and partners with him, and holds him back from these,

---

35 Literally: with hypocrisy toward.
36 Literally: race.
37 Literally: with hypocrisy toward.

not even letting him do a thing of righteousness, because the evil spirit opposes whoever wants to be faithful.[38]

Many are they of whom people boast because they are faithful and hasten to offer mercy to the needy; them too this spirit opposes. And others the spirit partners with in their works, so it spoils their fruits and cripples their progress. This is because they practice their virtues and offer mercy mixed with the glory of men. Men err in thinking that these have fruit, but they are like the bad sycamore tree which is thought to be full of sweet fruit when seen from afar, but when someone comes close to it, he finds nothing on it except rotten fruit which has no sweetness at all. And so are all who accept glory from men, for men think that they have abundant good fruits before the Lord, while they are devoid of fruit altogether. But God has left them in their aridity, and because He did not find good fruit on them, He deprived them of the great sweetness of His Divinity.[39]

3. But you, my children the strugglers, be diligent to stand face-to-face against the spirit of vainglory, oppose it, and prevail against it, so the power of God may come and help you, and abide in you, giving you vigor and fervor at all times. And I pray

---

38   Or: a believer.
39   The last sentence in *The Paradise of the Souls* is as follows: But God has left them arid for the sake of Him not finding in them good fruit, so He deprived them of the great sweetness of His Divinity.

The Third Letter

on your behalf too that this fervor may remain in you eternally, because it is true and there is nothing better than it. So if one of you sees that he does not have this fervor, let him ask for it diligently, and it will come to him. For it is like unto fire which, if men intend to boil some vegetables, they blow onto until it is kindled. And if it is kindled, the water acquires, through its heat, the nature of fire, and it boils bubbling up and is fiery.

And so, my brethren, if you see that your souls have grown cold through forgetfulness and negligence, be diligent to raise her [i.e. your soul] up and mourn over her, and then that fervor will come and unite with her and make her acquire its nature; therefore, she boils and bubbles up with good works. For David, when he saw he had grown heavy and cold, said, "I cast myself down before You, and remembered the days of old, and meditated on the works of Your hands,"[40] and also, "I spread out my hands to You; my soul thirsts for You like a waterless land."[41] Therefore, understand, my beloved, what David did, that when his heart grew heavy, he strove until the fervor set his heart on fire, so that he said, "My heart is ready, O God, my heart is ready."[42] His service, by night and by day, became light to him.[43] Do so also, that you may be gathered with

---

40 Cf. Psalms 142:5 LXX.
41 Psalms 142:6 LXX, OSB.
42 Psalms 107:2 LXX, OSB.
43 Literally: He became light in his service of the night and of the

readiness of heart in the light of the Divinity and its fire, and that God may reveal to you great ineffable mysteries.

And I ask Him that He may preserve your bodies, souls, and spirits whole until He carries you to the place[44] of His mercy, the place which our holy fathers have reached. Rejoice in the Lord, to whom is the glory forever and ever. Amen.

---

day. *The Paradise of the Souls* reads: And he received lightness in his service of the night and of the day.
44 Literally: residence.

THE FOURTH LETTER

To his children, the monks, urging them to acquire discernment because it is perfection

Know, my blessed children, that I write to you as to beloved children, worthy of blessing and the inheritance of the kingdom. Therefore, having become so, you should mention [in your prayers] night and day those who want to become children of the kingdom, that God may preserve them from all evils, and that they may consider all things [with discernment], meditate on what is good, and receive the good things prepared for the righteous.

And because you, my children, have become my beloved and children of the kingdom, I pray on your behalf unceasingly, that God may give you [the gift], to consider and discern all things, to distinguish between good and evil. For Paul the Apostle says, "Solid food is for the perfect, those who have exercised their senses and wills with much examination concerning good and evil,"[45] and they became children of the kingdom and were numbered in the divine adoption as sons. Therefore, God gives them this insight[46] and discernment in the rest of their works, so that they may not be deceived by men and the demons. And know that the enemy fights the believers under the pretense of good and deceives many, for they have not been given this insight and discernment.

2. And the blessed Paul, when he knew the riches which become the believers' and which are invaluable, wrote to the Ephesians who became his children and the children of the kingdom, for his great love for them, saying, "To the pure saints who are in Ephesus ... after I heard of your faith in our Lord Jesus Christ and your love for all the saints, I do not cease to give thanks for you, making mention of you in my prayers: that the God of our Lord Jesus Christ, the Father of glory, may give to you the spirit of wisdom and edification, that the eyes of your hearts may be enlightened; that you may know what is the hope of His calling and what are the riches of the glory of His inheritance in the saints."[47] And he also said, "I bow my knees to the Father, from whom the whole family[48] in heaven and on earth is named, that He would grant you, according to the riches of

---

45 Cf. Hebrews 5:14.
46 Literally: sight.
47 Cf. Ephesians 1:1,15–18.
48 Literally: fatherhood.

The Fourth Letter

His glory, that your conviction [i.e. faith] may gain health and power by what He strengthens you with through[49] His Spirit, that Christ may dwell in your inner man through faith, and in your hearts through love, your root and foundation being firm, that you may be able to comprehend with all the saints what is the width and length and height and depth."[50]

Look, my children, to the great Apostle, how he, upon knowing the greatness of these riches which were not known to those who were numbered of his children by their entrance into the faith, prayed for them that they might receive the knowledge of the greatness of this wealth, which he had known, which is the true insight,[51] that is, discernment, and there is nothing in the Christian faith that is greater than it. He asked this because of the greatness of his love for them, and his knowledge that if they receive it, nothing will be toilsome to them, and they will not be terrified by any fear, but the joy of our Lord will be their comfort night and day, and their labors will be sweet to them continually [and] at all times, and God will give them, for the sake of that, revelations of the great mysteries of the coming age, which we cannot describe with the fleshy tongue.

3. My beloved in the Lord, who have become my children, pray night and day, with copious tears,

---

49 *The Paradise of the Souls*: from.

50 Cf. Ephesians 3:14–18.

51 "Which is the true insight" appears only in *The Paradise of the Souls*. "Insight" is literally "sight."

for this insight and discernment, that the lasting good may be yours from our God, and [that] your comeliness may be increased in everything, and God may give you many other things you have not known at all. And I, your father, pray also for your sakes, that you may attain to this measure which is ours. For many of the monks and nuns who are in communities have not attained to this measure. And if you, my children, want to attain to this measure, which is perfection, stay away from all who carry this name which is of monasticism and virginity without having this insight and discernment. For if you keep company with them, they will not let you progress, but will quench your fervor, because they have no fervor but coldness, walking according to their will. If they come to you and speak words of this age with you and what is according to their will, do not agree with them, for it is written, "Do not quench the Spirit. Do not despise prophecies."[52] Know, my children, that the Spirit is not quenched in us except through vain talking, joking, and many other works which I cannot write one by one. If you see these people, do not despise them, but do good to them, and do not keep company with them lest they cause you to backslide.

And may the peace of our Lord come upon your meek spirits, my beloved children; He to whom [is due] praise and honor from the whole creation, forever and ever. Amen.

---

52   1 Thessalonians 5:19–20.

THE FIFTH LETTER

To his children, the monks; on love; and that he desires to see them, and that all may be comforted with what he makes known to them by word of mouth

1. Know, my beloved in the Lord, that the love of God continually visits our consciences and helps all who have prepared the thoughts of their hearts to remember[53] the church of the pure, night and day, without [their thoughts] stirring toward what is contrary to that. And as for those, the Holy Spirit is their unceasing remembrance, and He multiplies His prayers for their sakes, for they have become children to Him, in that He begot them in God; so [also] you whom I have considered my sons and have made sons of God, I do not cease from remembering you in my prayers night and day, that your faith may be firm and [that] you may abound in practicing[54]

---

53 Literally: the remembrance of.
54 Or: doing.

the virtues, and [that] our Lord may establish your insight and discernment, and give you a greater power than what you have. And this is my unceasing prayer for your sakes, forasmuch as I have begotten you in Christ, and you have become my sons. And so Timothy, when Paul the Apostle begot him in God and he became his son, he wrote to him likewise saying, "I remember you in my prayers night and day, greatly desiring to see you, being mindful of your tears, that I may be filled with joy, when I call to remembrance the genuine faith that is in you."[55]

2. Look, my children, to the Apostle, how Timothy became his son when he begot him in God. He used to do these three things for him: remembering him night and day, praying for him, and desiring to see him. In like manner, I am too, my beloved; for the sake of the uprightness of your hearts, my heart loves you. I do exactly what Paul did for Timothy, these three: I remember you, pray for you, and desire to see you. I do these because I remember your toils, your sighs, the sorrow of your hearts, the greatness of your patience, and your stillness. For you do all these with a strong heart and wisdom, for whoever does the works of God must do them with a spirit of wisdom. For so Paul the Apostle said, "For God has not given us a spirit of fear[56], but a spirit of wisdom and power of love."[57]

---

55 2 Timothy 1:3–5.
56 *Expanded Paradise*: spirit of failure.
57 Cf. 2 Timothy 1:7.

The Fifth Letter

And our Lord seeks from each of us that our works be [done] with this wisdom.

And now, my children, I beseech the Lord that He may facilitate my way to you once more, for I know that you desire to see me, as I all the more desire to see you. And know this, that on earth there is nothing that compares to the love of fathers for their children, and the [love of] children for their fathers; for they desire at all times to see each other. So if fathers and sons according to the flesh have this love, how much more do spiritual fathers and their children in God? They desire, with the fear of God and His love, to see each other. For the fathers in God are greater than the fathers according to the flesh, and the fathers' love for their sons is greater than the sons' love for their fathers. Therefore, the divine Apostle Paul said, "Though your love for me is slight, my love for you is great."[58]

Likewise, my children, I am your father, and my love for you is greater than your love for me. And because you have become my sons, let us pray together that our Lord may grant us to see each other once more. For I know that, by my meeting you, you will have gladness and joy, as Paul the Apostle said, "For I exceedingly long to see you, that I may impart to you the gift of the spirit, so that by it your assurance may be established, and [that] all of us may be comforted by my faith and your

---

58 Cf. 2 Corinthians 12:15.

faith."[59] For if we meet together, I will make known to you other things, [which] I cannot write to you in letters, that this may be to you a salvation in the Lord Jesus Christ, to whom is the glory, greatness, and praise, with His Father, and His Holy Spirit, forever and ever. Amen.

---

59 Cf. Romans 1:11–12.

THE SIXTH LETTER

To his children, the Monks, urging them to acquire the joy which the strugglers receive; and how they will judge the people of their generation who are negligent, on the Day of Judgement

1. You know, my beloved in the Lord, that within all of the rational creation, whether man or woman, there exists an inclination of love, to accept each of the spiritual[60] and carnal things.[61] For godly [men] love the spiritual things[62], and carnal [men] love the carnal [things]. And because the spiritual things[63] are in you, I love you with all my heart and spirit, for your acquisition of God in you, and with me your place has become great.

And I unceasingly beseech my God for your

---

60 Literally: things of God.
61 See Romans 8:5.
62 Literally: the divine things.
63 Ibid.

sakes, that the spiritual things[64] may grow in your hearts through His love, and that He may reveal to you the greatness of His mysteries, which I cannot express with my tongue because they are of the utmost loftiness and majesty, unlike those of this age. And they are not revealed to impure souls, but to those who have cleansed their hearts from all uncleanness and from the deeds of this passing world. Those are they who have despised the world, even their lives,[65] have carried the cross and followed the Lord in everything, and have done His will, so the spiritual things[66] dwelled in them and gave them sweetness and joy in God. And this joy nourishes[67] the souls and makes them increase in growth. And as the trees, if they do not take up of the nature of water, they cannot grow, so the souls, if they do not accept the heavenly joy, they cannot grow and ascend on high. But the souls who have accepted the heavenly joy can grow on high, for they have kept what we have previously said, and the mysteries of the kingdom of heaven have been revealed to them while [still] in the body. They have found boldness before God in everything, and He has fulfilled for her [i.e. the soul] all her requests.

2. And now, my beloved honorable [children], this is my perpetual entreaty: that you may attain to

---

64 "Spiritual things" is literally "things of God."
65 Literally: their souls or themselves.
66 Literally: the divine things.
67 *The Paradise of the Souls*: enriches.

The Sixth Letter

this degree and may know and realize the riches of the kingdom of God, which are immeasurable and infinite. And I know that no one is worthy of these riches except a few souls of the monks and virgins living in communities, because they have attained to the degree of perfection, and thrones have been prepared for them that they may sit on them on the Day of Judgment, to cast judgment.

And I know some in this our generation who have attained to this degree of being sons of God.[68] And there has not been a generation at all devoid of those who have attained to this degree, and neither will the coming generations too be devoid of these, not only of men but of women also. And if they sit on thrones, as was aforesaid, each of them will judge the people of their generation for having struggled until they were perfected, and the perfected are they who will judge the world. And this is what I pray for your sakes night and day, that you may attain to this degree, to judge the people of your generation. And what compels me to [do] that is my great love for you, which I am not able to explain through description, and neither can you, for Paul the Apostle says to those considered his sons, "I want to impart to you not only the gospel, but also our own selves, because you have become beloved to us in the Lord."[69] So, this is what I harbor in my heart for you, my beloved in the Lord.

---

68 Literally: degree of the sonship of God.
69 Cf. 1 Thessalonians 2:8.

And I have sent to you my beloved son in my place until God facilitates my coming to you in the body. And I will add unto you more joy than the joy you have, for the Lord, if He sees the father loving his sons, will Himself be joyful for them all, and will give them a great power and peace in the place of unity, which be the eternal kingdom, which is yours to inherit through the grace of our Lord Jesus Christ, to whom is the praise, glory, and majesty, forever. Amen.

THE SEVENTH LETTER

To his children, the monks, urging them on the perfection of obedience that the blessings of their fathers may come upon them

1. My beloved in the Lord, who have prepared yourselves for the kingdom of heaven and have sought God, so that what is your father's may be yours too, and that you may go to the place where your father is going, and that the blessing which comes upon him may come upon you, and the glory which he receives, you may receive—for you have become sons unto him, in the sonship of truth, blessing, and obedience. For the obedient children are they who inherit the riches of their fathers, their righteousness, and their blessing. And because the prayers which the sons offer before God are like the prayers of their fathers, they inherit, through them [i.e. the prayers], their virtues, their righteousness, and their blessings.

Thus were the prayers of Jacob like the prayers of his fathers in everything, and therefore all the blessings of his fathers came upon him, and he was worthy of beholding the spiritual ladder, and the angels ascending and descending on it. For before receiving the blessing of his fathers, he beheld not a single angel. And when he received their blessing, he saw the angels and was blessed by them. So did the true sons know that they cannot see any of the hosts unless they receive blessing from their fathers. And therefore they struggled in obedience and the asking of their fathers' blessing, that they may be worthy of beholding the angelic hosts, and through beholding them they stand fast in all matters without disturbance.

And so was the blessed Paul. When he saw them, he stood fast and was strengthened, and cried out, saying, "Who shall separate me from the love of Christ? Shall tribulation, or distress, or imprisonment, or persecution, or famine, or nakedness, or opposition, or sword? ... For neither death, nor life, nor angels, nor principalities, nor authorities, nor things present, nor things to come, nor powers, nor height, nor depth, nor any other lower creature, shall be able to separate me from the love of God, [which is] in Christ Jesus our Lord."[70] Therefore, behold, my beloved, that all who were diligent till they became dispassionate[71], care about

---

70 Cf. Romans 8:35–39.
71 Literally: without disturbance.

nothing at all, and so I would like you to be.

2. And I desire to see you because of your great love for God, and I beseech Him night and day, that the blessings of our fathers may come upon you, and my blessing too, I the poor one, that the intellectual powers may dwell in you, and you may pass the remaining days of your life with all gladness. For whoever has not reached this measure, has not reached the heavenly gladness yet.

And know, my children, that all the commandments are not burdensome nor toilsome, but [are] true light and eternal gladness, to him who has perfected obedience. And I say to you that I do not cease from praying for you that you may be with me where I am, for you have become my sons and have listened to me in everything. And our Lord Jesus Christ, when He saw that His disciples had listened to Him, besought His Father, saying, "Father, I desire that these be with Me where I am, for they have listened to My words and I give Myself up for them[72]. Father, You are in Me, and I in You, and they in Us, that they may be in oneness as We are."[73]

Therefore, behold, my children, the prayer of our Lord for His disciples, that they may be where He is, and His prayer to the Father also, that He may keep them from the evil one, till they reach the

---

72 "For them" is "for their sakes" in *Expanded Paradise*.
73 Cf. John 17:21–24.

places of rest, for they have become His beloved. And know that this also is my prayer to God for you, that He may protect you from the evil one, till you reach the places of rest, and that He may give you the blessing of our fathers. For these blessings, if they come upon you, will make a great grace abound in you. For Jacob, when he went to Mesopotamia after receiving the blessing, beheld the angels, and God blessed him for the sake of his obedience to his fathers and his receiving blessing from them. For when he beheld the angels face to face, he took hold of one of them till he received from him a blessing in abundance, and with it he blessed his sons. Likewise I the poor, beseech my God, whom I have served from my youth till now, that He may bless you and make you abound in blessing, that you may become, in your spirits and bodies, like our father Jacob, [who is] full of blessing.

3. And know that our father Jacob, when he was in Mesopotamia, remembered his parents and set about returning to his land, and he was afraid of his brother, so he offered him four gifts before meeting him. And his brother was not in need of that, for he was exceedingly rich. But he did this that he may dissolve the enmity that was between them, and [that] the blessing of his fathers may come upon him, for he had known of the power of the blessing of the fathers, as is written: "The blessing of the fathers comes upon the house of the children."[74]

---

74 Cf. Wisdom of Sirach 3:9.

The Seventh Letter

From now on, my beloved in the Lord, it is a joy to me that you mention my poverty, and mention also your father in the flesh, that their blessings may come upon you always. Know this, and may the peace of the Lord preserve your hearts, and His grace may support you, to whom be the praise from all rational beings, forever. Amen.

THE EIGHTH LETTER

To his children, the monks, informing them that fasting and the rest of the virtues are living, rational fruits, and that vainglory and the comfort of the body corrupt them and make them dead, evil fruits; and he urges them to flee from these and use those

1. Before all else, my blessed children, I ask God to give you the invisible [things], not these visible, "for the things that are seen are temporary [and] passing, but the things which are not seen are eternal [and] enduring."[75] This is my prayer [made] on your behalf because I have seen your fruits, [which are] living and rational, and you have become an inheritance and portion to God the Word; therefore, my heart has rejoiced exceedingly, because I know that God rejoices in those whose fruits are living and rational, and He makes them an inheritance and portion to

---

75 Cf. 2 Corinthians 4:18.

Himself.

All those, whose fruits are dead, are not counted [as] a portion to God, but He will blame them all the more, as He said to the prophet, to tell them this, by saying to him, "Cry out powerfully and have no pity, and lift up your voice like a trumpet and tell my people their sins and the house of Jacob their iniquities, because they are not far and will seek Me in the last days."[76] So they said, angrily, "Why have we fasted, and You have not seen? Why have we humbled our souls, and You have taken no notice?"[77] So He answered and said to those who said this, "For in the days of your fasting you are found to be doers of the evil will of your hearts, and those who are under your authority, you treat harshly and smite them on their heads. Your fasting is for judgment and wars, and you being so, I do not accept your fasting, because this is not the fasting which I chose, says the Lord."[78] He also said, "If you bend your neck like a ring, and put on sackcloth, and spread out ashes, this is not an acceptable fasting."[79]

Therefore, know, my children, that these are the dead fruits, and that God will not hear all those who do them when they entreat, but He would blame them all the more. The Holy Scripture showed this to us, by saying, "If therefore the light that is in

---

76 Cf. Isaiah 58:1–2.
77 Cf. Isaiah 58:3.
78 Cf. Isaiah 58:3–5.
79 Cf. Isaiah 58:5.

you is darkness, how great is that darkness!"[80] And the prophet says also in another place, "All your righteousness is like a menstrual rag to me."[81]

2. Therefore, since you, my beloved children, have known these dead fruits, care about none of them, lest your living and rational fruits become corrupted. And I pray to God for your sakes, that He may preserve your fruits from corruption, that He may make them grow, that your grace, your joy, and your love for the brethren and the poor may be multiplied, that He may perfect your good virtues and your true fruits until you go out of this habitation and gather with each other in that place where there is no illness, distress, nor evil, but joy, gladness, glory, garlands, crowns, pure fruits, the church of the pure, the inheritance that does not pass away, and the rest of the good things which "eye has not seen, nor ear heard, nor have entered into the heart of man."[82]

3. And I want you, my blessed children, to assist this prayer of mine and my immense love for you by persisting on [doing] the works of the Lord with steadfast hearts. And I beseech Him also that He may preserve you in this time from evil, and that you may be healthy in body, soul, and spirit, and that He may grant you knowledge in all matters to escape the tyranny of this age, and that you may

---

80 Matthew 6:23.
81 Cf. Isaiah 64:6.
82 1 Corinthians 2:9.

have peace and joy and salvation in the Lord, from these dead, evil fruits, the root of all of which is vainglory and the comfort of the body.

And may the peace of our Lord, Jesus Christ, come upon you all, He to whom is due glory, honor, praise, and veneration, with His Father and His Holy Spirit, now and always and unto the ages. Amen.

THE NINTH LETTER

On poverty and humility, with old and new testimonies; and he urges them on acquiring these to win the Kingdom

1. Let us, my beloved children, speak a little about the histories of the pure, saintly fathers, whom God lifted up for their humility and their first poverty, and He gave them glory and riches here, because they humbled themselves with all their hearts prior to God's exaltation of them.

We may first tell you about the patriarch Abraham, that God lifted him up from poverty to the riches, and from dishonor to glory; and all these were of the body[83]. And Abraham did not forget his first poverty, but rather he dwelt in tents. And Isaac and Jacob did likewise. It was possible for Abraham to build mansions for himself, everywhere, for he

---

83 This may mean in this physical world.

had acquired great riches, of gold and silver, of male and female servants, and of cattle. But since he knew that if his heart persevered in the remembrance of his poverty, he would not forget the many good things which God did with him. Therefore, he did not do that—that is, dwelling in mansions—but dwelt in tents. And therefore God appeared to him, with two angels, and he was sitting by the terebinth trees of Mamre.

And when he desired to care for our Lord and His two angels, he did not command one of his servants to do what he desired [to do], lest he forget the grace which He granted him after his humility and poverty. Rather he himself, in his good old age, which was nearly a hundred years, went to his herds, brought a good calf, and slaughtered it. And he commanded Sarah, his wife herself, to knead three measures of meal. And all their male and female servants were standing around them. And when Abraham offered them [the food] to eat, he was standing in their hands as a poor [person] who had no servants. For the sake of this poverty which he showed before the Lord, the Lord showed Himself to him and fulfilled to him all his will, and said to him on that day, "On this day next year, Sarah will have a son."[84] And it was so, and they were given Isaac.

2. Isaac also was exceedingly rich, but he became

---

84 Cf. Genesis 18:10 LXX.

poor in his heart, to the extent that the Philistines treated him unjustly as someone who was poor. As for him, he did not take revenge on them,[85] so his wealth increased more than theirs. And likewise Jacob, when he wanted to go to Mesopotamia, before the departure of his father Isaac, after he took his blessing, he abandoned much wealth and journeyed in his poverty, and he had nothing but his staff and sufficient food for the way. And he placed a stone under his head. Therefore, he became rich all the more in his uncle Laban's house. And when he wanted to return to his father's house, he did not forget his poverty because of the much riches which he possessed, for he always walked in poverty, but he even showed it before the Lord, saying, "I crossed over this Jordan with my staff, and now I have become two companies."[86] And see also how he did not forget his poverty even at the time of his departure.

And when he worshiped on the top of his staff, and his sons were around him, he commanded them, saying, "Do not forget your first poverty, my sons, because of these riches which have become yours."[87] And his staff was in his hand always, so that his heart may not become haughty by his exceeding riches when he looked at them, and [that] he may remember the servitude which he lived in his uncle

---

85 See Genesis 26:19–21.
86 Genesis 32:10 LXX, OSB.
87 According to the text.

Laban's house, for the staff was in his hand when he tended his flock of sheep.

And likewise Joseph, when he reigned over Egypt, did not forget his humiliation[88] and was not ashamed of revealing this to Pharoah, by saying to his brothers, "If Pharoah examines you, say to him, 'Your servants are shepherds.'"[89] He said this so that he may not receive honor from Pharaoh. Therefore, see how his reigning and riches did not make him forget his humiliation and poverty.

3. And likewise Moses, the arch-prophet, when he became a son to Pharoah's daughter and was given possession of all the treasures of Egypt,[90] he remembered his brethren, begotten of Abraham whom God lifted up from his humility and poverty. So he sought their life, and ran away from Egypt, and became a stranger in the land of Midian forty years. His bread and water were upon his shoulder while he herded the sheep. So when God looked to the abundance of his humility, He spoke to him, saying, "Return to Egypt and be a chief over the people of God."[91] Then Moses said to the Lord, "Look for someone else fitting for this matter, because I am not fitting for it."[92] Therefore, he angered the Lord by this saying; and his saying,

---

88 "His humiliation" is "himself" in *The Paradise of the Souls*.
89 Cf. Genesis 46:33–34 LXX.
90 See Hebrews 11:26.
91 See Exodus 3:10.
92 See Exodus 4:10.

of course, was in contempt for himself because he was never proud. And because of the greatness of his humility, God exalted him and gave him a sign in his staff, that he may not forget his poverty but confess the favor of its grace. And He commanded him to perform signs and wonders through the staff in his hand, and all the signs and wonders which the Lord performed with him were through his staff, that the remembrance of his poverty may be with him and he may not forget it, because of that staff which was always in his hand, with which he split the Red Sea and performed wonders in Egypt.

As for the sea, upon seeing the pillar of light which advanced before the people, it should have been split and should have turned running away, but this did not happen. Rather, God made Moses split the sea with his staff which was in his hand, so that if he became exalted because the sea was afraid of him, he would look to his staff in his hand and remember that it is the same staff with which he herded the sheep in the wilderness while he was a stranger and poor, so he would become humble. For Moses had this staff for two reasons: first, for his exaltation, because of the abundance of the wonders he performed through it; second, for the remembrance of his poverty, so that he may not become exalted in his heart, but say, "This power is not mine but the Lord's."

4. It was also said concerning Deborah that when she received from God that great dignity, that

The Ninth Letter

is, governing the entire people, her heart was not lifted up, but she would remember the custom of women and would consider that man is her head.[93] Therefore, when she desired to war against Sisera the King, she sent for Barak and gave him the authority to war against Sisera. As for Barak the righteous, this great honor did not lead him astray, neither did he forget God's dispensations, but he said to her, "If you will go with me, then I will go,"[94]—for he knew that God was with her and He had granted her the governance—though Deborah said to him, "If I go with you, you will not have glory, but it will be said that Sisera was delivered into the hand of a woman."[95]

Therefore, look, my children, to the honor of each of them. For Deborah could have said, "God has given me this honor and I will not give it to another," but she mentioned the custom of women because of the humility of her heart. And Barak also, when he took over the affair from Deborah, could have gone to war alone, that he may boast and say, "I have defeated Sisera," but rather he humbled himself that help may come to him from the Lord.

And likewise Gideon, when the Angel of the Lord said to him, "I send you to war against the King of Midian,"[96] his heart was not uplifted, but

---

93 See 1 Corinthians 11:3.
94 Judges 4:8 LXX, OSB.
95 Cf. Judges 4:9 LXX.
96 Cf. Judges 6:14 LXX.

he remembered his poverty and blamed himself in various ways[97], that he may rid himself of pride. Therefore, he first said, "Lord, by Your power, be with me, that Israel may be saved, for I and these multitudes are humiliated. And I am the youngest in my father's house [and my clan is the lowest] in Manasseh."[98] So the Angel said to him, "Go, and I will be with you."[99] But the humility of heart did not leave him without care; therefore, he asked for signs from the Angel, because he thought himself unworthy of this great measure, and for this [reason] he overcame Midian by the help of the Lord. And he would always remember his first poverty, fleeing from greatness. And when the people asked him to be ruler over them, he answered in humility of heart, "I will not rule over you, nor shall my son rule over you. The Lord shall rule over you."[100] And so he fled from rulership, and honor did not lead him astray at all.

5. And likewise Hannah, the mother of Samuel the prophet, made him a robe every year from her own [substance],[101] and it is known that the Temple of the Lord was not in need that the prophet's mother should provide for his clothes from her own [substance], but his mother did this because

---

97 Literally: kinds.
98 Cf. Judges 6:15 LXX.
99 Cf. Judges 6:16 LXX.
100 Judges 8:23 LXX, OSB.
101 See 1 Samuel 2:19.

he entered the Temple young, lest he says, "I am an angel or one of the powers, and I have seen revelations in the Temple." She used to do this yearly, so that he may know and be assured whose son he is and remember his humility and race. Therefore, he grew up, pleasing God exceedingly. And Hannah, his mother, too was humble and meek.

David also was humble and meek. Therefore, let us ourselves also, my children, take meekness and humility, like those, for David said, "Remember David, O Lord, and all his meekness."[102] And when he was herding his father's sheep, God chose him [to be] a king, more honored than all his father's house.[103] And when he went to fight Goliath, he took three stones from the brook and hid them in his shepherd's pouch, and he took his staff too with which he herded the sheep, and he advanced toward the mighty Goliath, and fought him, and defeated him by the Lord's power. He was brought before King Saul who gave him honor. But he did not give up his staff nor his shepherd's pouch, for the sake of the honor of the King's palace, but he kept them with him, that his heart may be always humble, and that he may also be an example to us to learn from.

And when he was anointed with the anointing oil and became a king, he said, "I have not forgotten my poverty and my humility, and have not become

---

102 Psalms 131:1 LXX, OSB.
103 See 1 Samuel 16:6–13.

exalted in my heart." He said concerning this, frankly, "O Lord, my heart is not exalted, neither are my eyes lifted up; neither have I walked in great things, nor in things too marvelous for me. If I were not humble, but lifted up my voice like a weaned child from his mother's milk, like the reward for my soul."[104] These psalms David did not say except after becoming a king, and he did not forget his first poverty, but said, "I was small among my brothers and the youngest in my father's house; I tended my father's sheep."[105] These words he said, that the whole world may know them and learn humility and poverty [through them].

Likewise Elijah the prophet also, after performing many wonders, did not give up his mantle, not [even] at his ascension to Paradise, lest his heart become exalted from the many signs which he performed, but after he ascended he cast it onto his disciple Elisha. He was also girded with a leather belt, that it may remind him that he was a poor man. And through his remembrance of this belt, he did not forget his first poverty.

6. And likewise the Apostles, when they began following our Lord Jesus Christ, used to always remember their first poverty, so when He was asked to pay the temple tax, our Lord said to Peter in Capernaum, "Go to the sea, cast in your hook, and

---

104 Cf. Psalms 130:1–2 LXX.
105 Psalms 151:1 LXX, OSB.

The Ninth Letter

take the fish that comes up first. And when you have opened its mouth, you will find a piece of money; take that and give it to them for Me and you."[106] Look, my children, how Peter did not leave his hook, lest he forget his humility and his poverty. Know that our Lord revealed these matters to us, so that we may humble ourselves[107], and that the devil may be exposed and disgraced, and that his flaming fiery darts may be quenched.[108]

Not only are these who are mentioned, and ones like them, the only ones who remembered their poverty, but our Lord Jesus Christ Himself was called the Son of David. And He said about Himself, "The Son of Man did not come to be served, but to serve."[109] And if they said to Him "You are the Son of God,"[110] He would rebuke the one who said this. And if he performed miracles and healings, He would command them saying, "Do not let anyone know."[111] In all this He humbled Himself for our sakes. He abandoned boasting not out of fear of it, no, because He is able to show the power of His Divinity whenever He desired. Rather this He did to teach us that we should preserve our poverty and our weakness, so as to behold the Lord and thereby

---

106 Cf. Matthew 17:27.
107 Or: so that we may be humble in ourselves.
108 See Ephesians 6:16.
109 Matthew 20:28.
110 See Mark 8:30; Luke 4:41.
111 See Mark 1:44.

we become humble, because it is evident that no one can become humble in the truth of his heart except the one whose soul has beheld the Lord.

7. And know, my children, that many seek with humility, and they are not so in the truth of their hearts. For they are in their appearance humble before men, and [yet] they have not beheld the honor of God. For this matter [inner humility] no one receives by much gold, silver, and copper; neither by seeking to be near an earthly king, nor his army; rather, it is mentioned concerning the pure, holy fathers that if they struggled and beheld the Lord, they would become all the more humble. For we heard written concerning Job that he said to the Lord, "Although You know, Lord, that I am not guilty[112], and there is no one who can deliver from Your hand."[113] "Would that there is a mediator between us for judgment,"[114] and the rest of the saying. When Job saw the Lord in the cloud and spoke with Him and [when] the eyes of his heart were opened and he beheld Him, he then considered himself dust and ashes[115], and he repented that he spoke with the Lord [in that manner], and said, "I lay my hand over my mouth. Once I have spoken, but I will not answer."[116]

---

112 *The Paradise of the Souls*: that I am a sinful man.
113 Cf. Job 10:7.
114 Cf. Job 9:33.
115 See Job 42:6.
116 Job 40:4–5.

The Ninth Letter

Likewise Isaiah the prophet also at first convicted the people of their sins, but after he saw the Lord of hosts and the seraphim standing around Him, he showed humility all the more, saying, "Woe is me, for I am a sinful man of unclean lips."[117]

And the disciples of our Lord Jesus Christ used to eat and drink with Him, and were not afraid when He conversed with them, but when He was transfigured on Mount Tabor and His form was changed before them, they fell on their faces, and knew their poverty, and became humble and learned that they are nothing before the glory of the Lord Christ. And we have many testimonies like this, but the cause of the greatness of the saints' humility is what they saw of the glory of God.

And what our Lord did with His disciples persuades us all the more, so that we may know that a soul obtains true humility in this world by her [i.e. the soul] seeing from afar the glory which it is to receive. For the Holy Scripture says, "Our Lord Jesus, knowing that the Father had given all things into His hands, ... rose from supper and laid aside His garments, took a towel and girded Himself. After that, He poured water into a basin and began to wash the disciples' feet, and to wipe them with the towel with which He was girded,"[118] for His disciples became humble.

---

117 Cf. Isaiah 6:5.
118 Cf. John 13:3–5.

8. And so, my beloved in the Lord, having beheld the glory of the Lord and known His inheritance which you will receive, cast away from you the glory of men and persevere in this great humility. And do not move from one place to another for the sake of men's glory, thereby you forget your first poverty. For I see people whose state[119] is such, and they seek men's glory, so if they obtain this in their communities, they move to other communities to obtain a greater measure of men's glory. Therefore, if you now know this, my children, do not move from a community to another for the sake of men's glory, but be in yourselves as infants and imitate the two disciples of John the Baptist, for they did not leave him with the purpose of boasting in another. Rather when they knew that the Lord Jesus was greater than John, through John's own testimony of Him, they followed Him to become of the new infants. You yourselves do likewise always when you go to the one who is greater than you, that what is written may be accomplished in you, "That your youth is renewed like the eagle's"[120]

9. Also say, "We are sinners," and weep for yourselves because of what you have done through lack of knowledge. And by this the will of the Lord will be in truth among you and working in you, for He is good and remits the sins of every man who returns to Him, and He does not remember them

---
119 Literally: image.
120 Psalms 103:5.

any longer. Rather He wants them themselves to remember their past sins, lest they forget them and thereby be held accountable for the sins which were remitted them. For so it happened to that servant whom his master forgave what he owed of talents, but when he forgot this and acted foolishly toward his fellow in servitude, the master required of him all that he owed, that is, what he had forgiven him, because he showed no mercy on his fellow in servitude, thereby forgiving him the hundred denarii which is a small amount in relation to that which was forgiven him.[121]

Moses also commanded His people in the wilderness not to forget their first sins, by saying to them, "If you entered the land which you would inherit, beware of eating and drinking and falling into pride, if you became rich, but remember your servitude in Egypt and also the things with which you angered the Lord in the wilderness. And this remembrance shall be yours throughout your lives."[122]

This teaching is for us, my children, having become servants for a long time in Egypt which is the sin that has enslaved us by our will. Let us strive, then, to enter the Promised Land, and if we entered, we should not forget our servitude but should always remember it, lest we eat and drink

---

121 See Matthew 18:24–34.
122 See Deuteronomy 8:11–14; 9:7; 4:9.

and fall into pride. And Moses is not the only one teaching us this, but also the rest of the prophets thus teach us, that we should not forget our sins which God has forgiven us and has forgotten them Himself. But we ourselves should remember them at all times, that we may be continually humble before the Lord, like a people appearing before a person whom they owe a debt.

Look to David the prophet also, who, when he sinned with Uriah's wife, and Nathan the prophet rebuked him for her sake and for the sake of what he did to her husband too, upon hearing the rebuke, he repented and humbled himself at once. For this [reason], Nathan said to him, "God has forgiven you your sins."[123] Nevertheless, when David received the forgiveness of his sins, he did not forget them, nor did he abandon their remembrance, but he wrote them in the fiftieth psalm,[124] and this became a remembrance in all generations, from generation to generation. When he received forgiveness, he said, "I will teach transgressors Your ways, and the ungodly shall turn back to You."[125] All this David said, that all sinners may learn from him and repent[126] like him, and that they may not forget their sins which were forgiven them; rather they ought to always remember them.

---

123 Cf. 2 Samuel 12:13.
124 According to LXX.
125 Psalms 50:15 LXX, OSB.
126 *The Paradise of the Souls*: arise.

And the Lord likewise said in the Book of Isaiah the prophet, "I blot out your sins and I will not remember them."[127] As for you, remember them that you may be purified. For this [reason], the sinner, if God forgave him his sins, must not forget them himself, but must remember them that he may be purified. The Lord also said to Jeremiah the prophet, "'Return to Me, all you house of Israel, that I may not bring My rebuke on you. For I am merciful,' says the Lord; 'I will not remain angry with you forever. Only acknowledge your iniquity,'"[128] and that you have become ignorant of yourself and hypocritical against your God. We likewise, my children, if our Lord forgave us our sins, ought not to forgive ourselves them, but ought to always remember them through the renewal of repentance. For this [reason], John the Baptist, when he baptized the people for the remission, commanded them, saying, "Do not be without care because of the remission of your sins, but bear fruits worthy of repentance, for even now the ax is laid to the roots of the trees. Therefore every tree which does not bear good fruit is cut down and thrown into the fire."[129] All these I have reminded you of, my beloved, because I remember the greatness of your virtue, and lest you become negligent and so your light becomes veiled; rather that your fruits may be increased, worthy of your

---

127 Cf. Isaiah 43:25 LXX.
128 Cf. Jeremiah 3:12–13.
129 Cf. Luke 3:8–9.

angelic Schema which you are wearing.

10. Know this also, how when that man found the treasure hidden in a field, he sold all his possessions and bought that field.[130] So you now, my beloved in the Lord, your glory has become manifest in all the cenobia, but do not dwell on this lest you become proud. Rather, by your humility and meekness, remember your first poverty, so you would become as someone who does not have knowledge of this. For Moses, when he was glorified, did not know of the splendor of his face, because of his humility and meekness. And when the people knew this and were greatly terrified to look at him, Moses covered his face.[131]

You likewise, my beloved, if you have left the good things of this passing world which is the land of the dead, as the aforementioned left it, let your hope be strong, that you may receive from the Lord the good things in the land of the living. And do not seek, my blessed children, to please the men who are in the region of the dead; otherwise you cannot please the Lord in the region of the living.

And if you obtained salvation from your sins, do not forgive yourselves on your part[132], lest the fruit of your repentance be infirm. Rather, imitate Paul the Apostle, the teacher of the world, who, after the

---

130 See Matthew 13:44.
131 See Exodus 34:29–33.
132 "On your part" is literally "alone."

Lord forgave him through His appearing to him and speaking with him, he alone did not forgive himself and did not forget his first foolishness which the Lord had forgotten through His mercy. Rather he said, "I persecuted the church of God,"[133] and [other] such examples.

May our Lord Jesus Christ keep you in His obedience forever, He to whom is due the sanctification and praise, with His Father and His Holy Spirit, now and always. Amen.

---

[133] 1 Corinthians 15:9 and Galatians 1:13.

THE TENTH LETTER

To his children, the monks, making known to them that true humility is not realized, except after beholding theoria which is the vision of God. He shows its three orders: the first, middle, and perfection, through old and new testimonies. Also he urges them to fulfill this through the help[134] of God.

1. Know, my beloved, that an ascetic is not the one who is steadfast in one thing [of righteousness]; nor is the one who clings to one thing [of evil] is the adversary of virtue. And if asceticism is the glory of virtue, then many evils oppose it. The one who desires to be perfect in asceticism must not be enslaved to anything of evil. For the one who is enslaved to one thing of evil is far from the degree of perfection, for perfection as it was said is: "I am

---

134 *The Paradise of the Souls*: knowledge.

free from all [men], that I might win the more."¹³⁵ This saying Paul the Apostle said because he did not make himself a servant to evil, and because he did not go back to what he had left behind.¹³⁶ And when he was liberated from evil and was set free from it finally, he prayed for the sake of the benefit of the many who wanted to become enslaved to evil, because they were not able to rid themselves of the sin of their evils. For they are incapable of the power of the saying of the psalm, "Let us break their bonds in pieces and cast away their yoke from us."¹³⁷

When Paul the Apostle beheld the Lord Jesus, he obtained perfection¹³⁸, and then he became a support for those who had no strength, that they may reach perfection and go to the height; and this [is] through the greatness of humility which became his, after the pattern of our Lord Jesus Christ who hid His Divinity by His humanity through the greatness of His humility. For He was looked at as a Man while He was not a Man only, but God who became Man, as it is written, "And the Word became flesh and dwelt in us."¹³⁹ Paul the Apostle likewise, when he walked in humility as the Lord commanded him, said, "I became to those who are without law, as

---

135 Cf. 1 Corinthians 9:19.

136 Last clause is the following in *The Paradise of the Soul*: he did not teach himself what he had left behind.

137 Cf. Psalms 2:3.

138 *The Paradise of the Souls*: perfection happened to him.

139 Cf. John 1:14.

without law (though I was not without a law), that I might win those who are without a law."[140] The Apostle did not, by this, abandon[141] his perfection. Neither did our Lord abandon His Divinity by His incarnation which was necessary [for our sakes],[142] as it was said in the Law and as it was written in the Gospel that "the Word became flesh and dwelt in us."[143]

And the Apostle was perfect[144] because, firstly, he was liberated from every evil; secondly, he was not enslaved to any of the desires, for he became an ascetic; and finally, he was set free by beholding the Lord Jesus Christ. And when he saw Him, he at once followed His sayings without delay, and he became utterly perfect and humble. And likewise all those who cling to the Lord's sayings, shall know the truth and the truth shall make them free and shall liberate their souls of every evil, as Paul the Apostle became so, because our Savior made him free. Therefore, he said about himself, "Am I not free? Have I not beheld the Lord as those first [Apostles] beheld Him?"[145]

2. Many say in their foolishness, "We have seen the Lord Jesus like the Apostles." My children,

---

140 Cf. 1 Corinthians 9:21.
141 Literally: become outside.
142 The phrase in brackets appears only in the *Expanded Paradise*.
143 Cf. John 1:14.
144 Literally: was in his perfection.
145 Cf. 1 Corinthians 9:1.

those are deceived and have gone astray and have no eyes with which to behold as the Apostle beheld the Lord. For the Apostle saw the Lord as He was seen by the Apostles who were with Him and those who believed in Him at that time when He was walking and the crowds were around Him, where they saw Him as a Man. And the woman who had a flow of blood, having beheld Him with the eyes of her heart, believed that He is God and by faith[146] touched the hem of His garment, and so she was saved. Then the Lord said, "Who touched Me?" not that He did not know, but so that He may make her faith known. Therefore, Peter said to Him, "The multitudes throng You, and You say, 'Who touched Me?'" And when the woman showed that she was healed, the Lord said to her, "Go in peace; your faith has saved you."[147]

As for Pilate, Annas, and Caiaphas, they saw the Lord like the rest of the multitudes who used to behold Him with the bodily eyes only. And because they did not behold Him by faith as the Apostle beheld Him, therefore they did not benefit at all from seeing Him. The Apostle, however, beheld Him with the eyes of his heart and by his strong faith, as the woman who had a flow of blood beheld Him, who touched Him by faith, so she was healed. And as our Lord Jesus Christ appeared to His Apostle Paul after he overcame the passions, and He made

---

146 "By faith" appears only in *The Paradise of the Souls*.
147 See Luke 8:43–48.

him free, so everyone who has become liberated from the passions, will behold the Lord with the eyes of his heart and become free. But he will not be able to behold with his bodily eyes that exceedingly glorious light which Paul the Apostle beheld.

As for those who are deceived [and] proud of themselves, their evil is great. They cannot receive the Bread of Life, because their eyes are not full of light, and they are not pleasing to God, whom all the pure worship and see Him with their hearts[148]. For our Lord appears to such as those who are not servants to the passions, for so it is written about Isaiah the prophet that the Lord ceased to appear to the prophet because he did not rebuke King Uzziah, and prophecy was withheld from him. And after the death of Uzziah, the angel of the Lord appeared to him and cleansed him by the live coal and the fiery tongs.[149]

3. Know then, my beloved, that the man, in whom the authority of sin has died, God appears to his soul and purifies it, together with the body. If the authority of sin were still alive in the body, it would not be possible for the man to behold God, because his soul dwells in darkness, and it is impossible for the light, which is the vision of God, to appear in it. For David the prophet says, "In Your light,

---

148 *The Paradise of the Souls*: whom all the pure worship in their hearts and see Him.
149 See Isaiah 6:6.

Lord, we see light."[150] So what is this light, in which man sees God? It is the light which our Lord Jesus Christ mentioned in the Gospel, that man ought to be full of light, having no part dark.[151] As He also said, "Nor does anyone know the Father except the Son, and the one to whom the Son wills to reveal Him."[152] And the Son, my children, does not show His Father to the sons of darkness, but to those who are steadfast in the light, who are the sons of light; and He has illuminated the eyes of their hearts by the knowledge of the commandments.

Therefore, we must first imitate Moses, the great among the prophets, so that we may find the glory of his faith in God who is invisible. For Moses became a son to Pharoah's daughter, and when he chose to labor with the people of God, he cast away from himself the servitude [which is] full of humiliation. And he had not beheld God yet, being [still] in servitude, but when he was saved from Pharoah's servitude, he was set free and became worthy of beholding the bush, [which was] burning with fire and was not consumed. And it was said that it was a great vision. This was a beginning to him; then he beheld the middle mystery, and perfection was after that.

This Moses, when he left Egypt and fled from Pharoah, was forty years [of age] at that time. He did

---
150 Cf. Psalms 36:9.
151 See Luke 11:36.
152 Matthew 11:27.

something contrary to Pharoah; then he was alone in the wilderness of Midian, which is interpreted "The Place of God." For the intellect, if it separates from the many [people] and becomes [living] in solitude, God strengthens and confirms it, so that it may be able to ask and search for the things of the Lord. And thereupon it beholds the greatness of His power and His Divinity and His beauty[153] in His creation.

Therefore, my children, the beginning of the great vision is the first look which Moses took[154] while he was marveling at the bush which was burning and was not consumed. And this looking is far from the degree of perfection. As for beholding the middle mystery, it is that he advanced more than the first [degree] and said, "I will now turn aside to see this great sight.[155]" And when he advanced, the Lord called him. Perfection, however, is his humility after God spoke to him, and [after] he saw Him, and [after] he performed signs.

4. And know, my children, that these visions[156], which are of God, with respect to those who are not perfect, are as those looking in a mirror. As for those who have reached perfection, the eyes of their hearts are unveiled, and a great light appears to them, with ease, not with labor. For nothing remains of the

---

153 Or: glory.
154 Literally: looked.
155 Cf. Exodus 3:3.
156 Or: sights.

rebuke of sin and darkness in the eyes of the perfect. For these two, if they were present in the heart, would not let the soul behold with the perfection belonging to the perfect, which is the beholding which belonged to Paul the Apostle and his likes, of which the Apostle said, "We all, with unveiled face, beholding as in a mirror the glory of God, are being transformed from glory to glory."[157]

Likewise Moses the prophet did not change from one place to another and from one region to another, but his change was apparent, marvelous, for he beheld this great vision, that is, the fire burning in the bush without it being consumed and then God speaking to him[158]. For this is the marvelous change which is a type of the marvelous, incomprehensible mystery. And this is the change which Paul the Apostle mentioned that it is a change "from glory to glory," and from faith to [a greater] faith, and from a deficient virtue to a perfect virtue. For this change and progress are what bring us near to the Lord, so we receive the vision[159] of the knowledge of His strength. For God says on the mouth of His prophet, "Those near to Me will know My strength."[160] Therefore, if the one who comes near to God knows His strength, then the one who does not come near to Him will not know His strength.

---

157 Cf. 2 Corinthians 3:18.

158 *The Paradise of the Souls* adds here: and the sight [or vision].

159 Or: beholding.

160 Cf. Isaiah 33:13 LXX.

As for the intellect, which has not come near to God yet, the hypocrite—that is, the devil—will lift it up like the cedars of Lebanon. So if the intellect comes near to God, and unites with Him, and becomes one with Him, the hypocrite then will no longer appear to the one whom he used to lift up at first. And concerning this, David the prophet teaches us, saying, "I saw the hypocrite greatly exalted and lifting himself up like the cedars of Lebanon; and I passed by, and behold, he was not; and I sought for him, but his place was not found."[161] David the prophet did not seek the hypocrite nor his place, except for his search for the knowledge of God, and for this [reason] he did not find the hypocrite at all. And his saying "I passed by" is as his saying in another psalm, "I shall pass through in the place of the wondrous tabernacle, to the house of God."[162] For this passing through, which is passing by, reveals to us the growth of the soul, for the prophet gave it [as] the sign of perfection, for before, its way was far from God.

5. Do not marvel, my children, in that our way is still far from God. This is because we are still in spiritual infancy. For we see that it was said to the great prophet Elijah, "Arise, and eat and drink, and be strong, because the way is far for you."[163] And concerning this remoteness, David the prophet

---

161 Cf. Psalms 36:35–36 LXX, OSB.
162 Cf. Psalms 41:5 LXX.
163 Cf. 1 Kings 19:7.

The Tenth Letter

said, "Who will give me wings of a dove, that I may fly away and be at rest?"[164] And by these we must learn that the life of each of us is needy, and the way arduous. Therefore, we should not strive with weakness, slackness, and negligence, but with restraint and steadfastness. For the teacher of the world, Paul the Apostle advises us that "we ought to press on, that we may lay hold,"[165] and also says, "I discipline my body and bring it into subjection."[166]

Let us run now, my children, so long as there is time for us in this body, that we may lay hold of perfection, which St. Paul laid hold of, saying, "I have fought the good fight, I have finished the race, I have kept my faith. From now, there is laid up for me the crown of righteousness."[167] When this Apostle laid hold of perfection, while in the body, he longed to depart from it, and said:

> And I too, if I had in my life in the flesh fruit of my labor, what I shall choose I cannot tell. For I am hard-pressed between the two, having a desire to depart and be with Christ, which is better for me and more beneficial. Nevertheless I am obliged to remain in the flesh, for the sake of your gladness and the raising of your faith. Only let your conduct

---

164 Cf. Psalms 54:7 LXX.
165 Cf. Philippians 3:12.
166 1 Corinthians 9:27.
167 Cf. 2 Timothy 4:8.

be worthy of the gospel.[168]

Likewise, therefore, you also do, my children, for everyone who pursues with negligence and laziness, his end will overtake him before becoming perfect in Christ. As Solomon said in the Proverbs, "The souls of the lawbreakers will be taken away from them before they reach the fear of God."[169] So it happened with King Hezekiah[170] when the end of his days overtook him while in heedlessness. When he repented[171] from what he was, and prayed to the Lord, he became worthy of additional years, and he grew increasingly. And when these years were fulfilled, his soul departed from his body, while he was in the utmost perfection of the service of God.

6. Know this also, just as the body has three measures during the period of time when the soul is in it, which are youth, manhood, and old age, so too the soul has three measures, hidden in the body, which are the beginning of faith, work, and perfection. First, if a soul begins to believe, then it is born in Christ as the Gospel said.[172] And John the Apostle gave us a sign too for this birth, its middle [stage], and its perfection, by saying, "I write to you, little children.... I write to you, young men....

---

168 Cf. Philippians 1:22–27.
169 Cf. Proverbs 10:27.
170 2 Kings 20:1–11; Isaiah 38:1–8.
171 Literally: returned.
172 See John 3:3.

I have written to you, fathers..."[173] This writing is not for his beloved who are of the body, [that is, not according to the statures of the body], but to the believers in their three measures, who "desire the pure milk of the word,"[174] who advance toward perfection, who are worthy of the true grace. And for this [reason], when David the prophet learned the measure of the days of the perfection of the soul here, and that he had advanced in his days in the body, and that he was near to be loosed from it, and that he did not have those days of the soul, he asked God, saying, "Lord, do not take me away in the midst of my days."[175] This care of his was with respect to the spiritual days, not bodily days. For the meaning of his saying "in the midst of my days" is his dread that his soul be taken from him before the completion of his days, and he be a stranger to perfection.

And it was likewise testified of Abraham too that he grew old and became advanced in his days. Likewise all the pure, after believing, used to weary their bodies, to humiliate them, for their humiliation of their bodies prepared for them an old age in the growth of worship and the service of God.

7. Likewise understand, my children, the matter of Daniel and how he became a child in his flesh and an old man in his mind, not like the two old

---

173 1 John 2:12–14.
174 1 Peter 2:2.
175 Cf. Psalms 101:25 LXX.

men who were advanced in their days in the flesh, while in their deeds were like children, and the lust of youth[176] was with them; these two were rebuked by the pure words of the youth Daniel, regarding their fleshly, childish old age, and he judged them concerning the righteous saint Susanna, saying to them, "O you who have become advanced in their evil days,"[177] and the rest of the saying.

8. Likewise Joseph also, whoever loves asceticism ought to imitate his purity and chastity, and ought to begin training himself on recitation [that is, rumination], and ought to prevail against all the lusts of the flesh, for they are contemptible. And then he can trample upon the other strong lusts which are of the cunning enemy, and say as Job the righteous said, "Power has vanished from his loins and the center of his stomach."[178]

In truth, my children, everyone who struggles and prevails against the lusts of the flesh, which are generated from the abundance of foods and drinks, can gird up his loins with chastity, and refresh his heart with the saying of the psalm: "Gird Your sword upon Your thigh, O Mighty One."[179] The meaning of this saying is that the word of God, with which chastity is acquired, is "sharper than any two-edged

---

176 Or: childhood.
177 Cf. Daniel Susanna:52 LXX, OSB.
178 Cf. Job 40:16 LXX.
179 Psalms 44:4 LXX, OSB.

sword,"[180] as the Apostle says. This sword is capable of cutting off and killing all the evil desires.

And likewise Jacob too, when an Angel wrestled with him, He drew a sinew from his thigh. Therefore, his body failed and became weak, and he was called "Israel," which means "Wrestled with God."[181] And we too likewise ought to weaken the body, with wisdom and guidance, that the lusts may be weakened and quenched. And this weakness completes in us the power of chastity, and concerning this weakness the Apostle says, "For when I am weak, then I am strong."[182]

David the prophet also boasted in this weakness, by his saying, "There is no healing in my flesh."[183] He said this because he had weakened his body nobly, for he was seeking the great salvation. For this is not a lack of healing, but [rather] it is healing and salvation, because if the body is weakened, then the soul is strengthened. So let us, then, weaken our bodies, with wisdom and guidance, so that we may be able to restrain ourselves, because if we suppress the body and bring it under the subjection of the soul, then the fleshly thoughts, whose love is enmity with God[184], will die through that weakness; then

---

180 Hebrews 4:12.
181 See Genesis 32:25. "The beholder of God" appears in the *The Paradise of the Souls*.
182 2 Corinthians 12:10.
183 Psalms 37:4 LXX, OSB.
184 See James 4:4.

the soul shines and becomes a temple of the Holy Spirit.

9. The one who strives to become pure[185] in all his members, this one is the true ascetic, and is not an adulterer. And he can say with David the prophet, "All my bones shall say, 'O Lord, who is like You?'"[186] This is the one who has trained[187] all his senses and has not permitted them to have dominion over him; and he has fixed them and placed upon them the yoke of the Lord through the greatness of purity. For he will not let his eyes behold anything that is not good, nor to desire a woman; neither will he let his ears hear slander nor the counsel and thoughts of the devil. Therefore, in him is fulfilled that which is written, "Your ears were not inclined to vain words."[188] These words made him worship Christ all the more, as a fragrant oil and sweet-smelling incense. And his mouth also, he kept watch over it[189], and did not permit it to be devoted to foolish speech. And his hands, he made them work, with no injustice [or deceit], good deeds with mercy and truth. And his feet did not pursue the shedding of blood, but [rather] hastened earnestly toward the saying of the Lord, "And whoever compels you to

---

185 Or: chaste.
186 Psalms 35:10 LXX, OSB.
187 Literally: taught.
188 Cf. Psalms 140:4 LXX.
189 Cf. Psalms 140:3 LXX.

go one mile, go with him two."[190] And his belly and chest, he kept watch over them, so that he does not fall through them upon the earth like the serpent which moves on its belly and chest.

10. This, my brethren, is the attribute of the ascetic. As for those who are not ascetics but rather who rise early to drink intoxicating drinks, we hear regarding them the saying of the prophet, "They burn through their intoxication by wine, and their eyes they give to the handling of cups. They eat the best of the herds of the sheep and calves, and the sucklings from the yoke of oxen. They delight in soft beds and take pleasure in whatever is carnal."[191] And they consider themselves wise, while they are enemies and dragons, because the dragon works in them, having cast their bellies and chests down on to the earth. And they think themselves to be intellectual and to have the knowledge of books, and [yet] they teach them in an evil way, because they are chests for the dragon.

Know this, my children, that these, whom the prophet spoke of[192], are the ones who introduce strange beliefs into the true doctrines and upright faith. And they oppose the strong, firm faith by their false, unstable faith, saying concerning the Creator of all things that He is created, not knowing that God created everything by His Word, as St. John

---

190 Matthew 5:41.
191 Cf. Amos 6:4–6.
192 Literally: meant.

the Evangelist testified, saying, "In the beginning was the Word, and the Word was with God, and the Word is God.... All things were made through Him, and without Him nothing was made that was made."[193] Therefore, if it has been confirmed that all things were made through Him—the heavenly and the earthly, the visible and invisible—as the Creed testified, how do these dare to say about Him, after His union [with the body], that He is as one of the creatures, by their saying that Christ is created? For these are the ones who made the chest of their heart confined under the dragon's chest, as the saying of the prophet stated in advance concerning them, that the dragon strives in their chests and bellies.

My children, as for those who raised their minds from the earth, looking to heaven where Christ is sitting at the right hand of God, they have become foreign to[194] the belly and its lusts. And our Lord Jesus Christ, the one essence, the one hypostasis, the one nature, and the one will, receives them and presents them to His Father as good and choice things.

11. Therefore, having known this, my beloved, let each one of us, who desires to be ascetic, endeavor to stay away from the multitudes and refrain from coming near them, so that he remains in body and heart and mind foreign to the turmoils of the

---

193 Cf. John 1:1, 3.
194 "Foreign to" is also "outside of."

multitudes and fellowship [with them]. For there is great turmoil among the people. And our Savior Jesus Christ became to us an example of staying away and solitude, by going to the mountain alone to pray; and also [an example to us by] His defeat of Satan in the desert when he warred against Him. And this is not because of His inability to defeat him amidst the many [people], but so that He may teach us that through solitude and stillness we can defeat our enemies and lay hold of perfection. Likewise our Savior did not reveal His glory to His disciples before men, but took them and went up into the mountain and showed them His glory. And John the Baptist also was in the desert till the day of his manifestation to Israel.

Know also, my children, that our enemy has intensified [his war] against us by his visible and invisible weapons, and that he has made some men an instrument and a weapon, because of their obedience to him. And through these, he opposes the believers. He made them like the unchaste woman whom he took [as] a powerful weapon, because she spreads her wings with a daring heart. And Peter the Apostle also teaches us the benefit of solitude, because when he was alone [praying], he beheld the heaven open and a sheet descending upon him, and God spoke to him concerning it. Afterwards the sheet was lifted up from him to heaven.[195]

---

195 See Acts 10:9–16.

12. Likewise Ezekiel the prophet, when he saw the four-faced four living creatures with the wheels, which indicate the glory of God, this was not in a city or village, but outside in the field, for God said to him, "Go out into the field and there you shall see My glory."[196] And in general, these visions and revelations the saints did not obtain except in the mountains and deserts.

Paul the Apostle also spoke about these saints and their honorable life in his epistle to the Hebrews, saying, "They wandered in deserts and mountains, in dens and caves of the earth."[197] The prophet also, when he learned that solitude pleases God, said, "It is good for a man to bear the yoke of the Lord in his youth. Let him sit alone."[198] David the prophet also said, "I am alone, until lawlessness passes away."[199] Jeremiah the prophet too, because of his knowledge of the disturbance which is amidst the multitudes and that it troubles those who desire to please God, did not refuse to say, "Oh, that I had in the wilderness a lodging place; that I might leave this people, and depart and be far from them!"[200]

Learn[201], my children, the virtue of solitude. For our Lord Jesus Christ, through His going into

---

196 Cf. Ezekiel 3:22.
197 Hebrews 11:38.
198 Cf. Lamentations 3:27–28.
199 Cf. Psalms 56:2 LXX.
200 Cf Jeremiah 9:2.
201 Or: know.

solitude many times, gave us a firm hope in the love of solitude, as David the prophet said, "For You alone, O Lord, cause me to dwell in hope."[202] And Elijah the prophet also, who was worthy of the spiritual food and of being fed by the angel of the Lord, this did not become his in the midst of the multitudes, in a city nor in a village, but in the desert only.

All that belonged to the saints, of these and such like it, "were written for our admonition,"[203] that we may become jealous of them, those who loved solitude which can bring us to the Lord, for it is a great consolation and makes a person perfect. Those who loved solitude with all their hearts and with all their souls, a greater honor and light became theirs, more than those who dwell in cities and villages. Therefore, be diligent then, my beloved children in the Lord, to remain steadfast in it, as is ought, that it may bring you to beholding God, which is the spiritual vision of God[204], by the grace of our Lord and God and Savior Jesus Christ, to whom is due glory from all rational [beings], with His good Father and His Holy Spirit, now and forever. Amen.

---

202 Psalms 4:9 LXX, OSB.

203 1 Corinthians 10:11.

204 Literally: *theoria*.

THE ELEVENTH LETTER

To his children, the monks, informing them that if they reached divine visions and revelations, they ought to be on their guard against demonic visions, lest they go astray through their false deceptions, and their hearts become exalted. And he urges them to continue in obedience.

1. Know, my beloved children, that from the beginning, when the soul deviated from the commandment, the disobedience occurred, and through the disobedience, all souls were taken to Hades, as the Apostle said, "By the first man [or first Adam] came death."[205] Then God the Word had compassion and became incarnate of us through the incomprehensible mystery, and He fulfilled all the economy for our salvation. So He descended into Hades and led it captive, and drew from it

---

205 Cf. 1 Corinthians 15:21.

all the souls who were imprisoned in it, and saved them from the dominion of the devil, and kept by His order—not by the authority of the devil—the disobedient in the darkness until the awesome Day of Judgment, and lifted up, to heaven where Paradise is, those who by their will obeyed, listened, and performed the divine orders. The reason for lifting them up to heaven is the invisible fire which was kindled in their hearts, which is the fervor of good works.

2. And not only do I make this known to you, but also [I make known] what this soul resembles in which the fire of God has dwelt. It resembles a bird having two wings, with which it flies and soars high in the heaven. For the birds, apart from all the creatures, were granted wings. And the wings of the soul of the worshipper of God are the power of the fire of God, with which [the soul] can fly to the height of heaven. Therefore, if the soul were deprived of these wings, it no longer would have the ability to soar in the air, because it lost the power of that fire. It is like the bird whose wings were plucked out, and so it became unable to fly.

The soul of man also resembles a bird, in that fervor [or heat] is the cause of his existence in the world. For if the bird does not incubate its eggs at all times, live chicks cannot hatch out of them, for their lives cannot exist except through heat. And for this [reason] the Lord said in the Holy Scripture, "O Jerusalem, Jerusalem, the one who kills the prophets and stones those who are sent to her! How often I wanted to gather your children together, as a hen gathers her chicks under her wings."[206]

Now that you have understood, my children, the analogy between birds and the soul of the worshipper of God, the origin of whose existence is heat [or fervor]. Therefore, let not the power of this fire be taken away from you, for many wars will be [waged] against you by the devil because of this fire which the Lord has given to you, so that he may take it away from you. For he knows that he has no power over you as long as this power is with you and in you.

3. Struggle then against him, and know his deceits and tricks, for he hides his bitterness in sweetness so that it is not made manifest. And he portrays to you many things as good, and they are not so, that he may incline your hearts to him through his tricks which are in the likeness of truth. For this is his craft always, to resist, with all his might, all the souls who worship[207] God in a good a manner. And he casts many [and] diverse passions into the soul, to quench that fire, through which—and from which—virtue is established. Foremost in this is the comfort of the body and what belongs to it. If the devil saw that he is not obeyed, and his order was not received at all, he would come up with other

---

206 Matthew 23:37.
207 Or: serve.

tricks in the form of righteousness, so he appears as "an angel of light,"[208] as Paul the Apostle said; then [he would come up] with other things greater than this, to incline their hearts to him. Therefore, if he saw that they also restrained themselves from these other things, and they did not accept them from him nor did they listen to him at all, then he would turn away from them in shame. And then the Spirit of God dwells in them. Therefore, if the Spirit of God dwells in them, He gives them rest in all their labors and sweetens the taking of the yoke of God for them, as it was written in the Scripture, "Take My yoke upon you."[209] And so they endure and do not become wearied at all in practicing the virtues, nor in the service [of God], nor in keeping night vigils; and they are not angered by the insult of men and are not afraid of any man at all, nor of a beast, nor of poverty, nor of evil spirits, for the joy of God abides in them night and day, nurturing their minds and nourishing them. For the soul is continually nurtured by this joy and is nourished by it, and [the soul] through it ascends to heaven.

4. And as the figure and stability of the body are [sustained] by bread and water and such things like these, from the beginning of his life to its end, we see that an infant is brought up by his mother's milk, then by soft food, and afterwards by what comes his way day by day. And so he is strengthened, and

---

208 2 Corinthians 11:14.
209 Matthew 11:29.

his heart is emboldened against his enemies who oppose him. Therefore, if an illness befalls him, which prevents him from receiving nourishment, his enemies prevail against him from every side and overcome him, and he cannot be healed of his illness and overcome his enemies except by a physician who remains with him and treats him. [As the body], so is the soul of man; if the joy of God is not in her, she is found to be ill and ridden with malignant wounds. Therefore, if she is diligent in seeking a man who is a servant of God and who has knowledge of the spiritual medicine, and she clings to him, he heals her of her passions first; then she rises again, so he teaches her the matters of God. And in this manner she regains that joy, which is her food. And then she can counteract her enemies, which are the evil spirits, and overcome them, and trample upon their counsels; and she becomes perfected by joy.

5. Therefore now, my beloved, having learned this, be on your guard against the evil counsels of the devil, for he comes in the form of one who says the truth, to deceive and tyrannize those who accept him. So if he comes to you as an angel of light, do not believe him or listen to him, because he hunts the believers through ways that seem good, yet are not so. And those who have not attained perfection yet, do not know these wiles of the devil, nor what he casts into them at all times. As for the perfect, they know them, and as the Apostle said, "But solid food belongs to those who are perfect, that is, those

who have their senses and determinations exercised, and have learned to discern good from evil."[210] Those the enemy is not able to tyrannize.

As for the believers who are not perfected yet, if they do not stand guard over themselves, he deceives them with his food which is good in appearance and [yet] is not so, and he lures them as the fisherman [lures] the fish after concealing the head of the hook with the bait. Therefore, the fish, because they do not know of the hook hidden with the bait, advance and swallow the bait, and so they are caught at once and easily. Therefore, understand this, that if the fish had known that they would be caught by that bait, they would have fled away from it and would not have approached it to begin with. Thus, as we said concerning the believers who are not perfect, the enemy hunts them through reasons that resemble the truth. As Solomon the wise says, "There is a way that seems right, but its end leads to the lowest depths of hell."[211]

It is also written in Amos the prophet, "'Amos, what are you doing here?' So he said, 'I see a snare to catch the bird.'"[212] And it is known that the bird, out of fear of being caught on the earth, soars high in the air and makes its dwelling in high places, for its rest and sleep. Therefore, if it slept, it would be without worry, for no one can reach it to catch it.

---

210 Cf. Hebrews 5:14.
211 Cf. Proverbs 16:25.
212 Cf. Amos 8:2 LXX.

We may see that the hunter acts with deceit, and comes below its dwelling and sets his snare and deceives it with a bait. By this, he brings it down from its height and snatches it.

Likewise does the devil do, and he catches the believers who are not perfect, with his wiles which resemble the truth and [yet] are not so, and he brings them down from their height. For so did the devil do, when he hid [himself] in the serpent, and said to Eve, "If you eat of the tree, you will be gods, and your eyes will be opened."[213] So when Eve heard these words, her heart was inclined to them, and she supposed them to be true, for she did not examine them. When she ate and gave Adam to eat, the great shame befell them, and they both fell from their height.

6. So does the devil do with the believers who have not attained perfection yet, when they do not discern between good and evil, but they follow their passions and are persuaded by their opinion, and they do not return to learn from their fathers who have been perfected and have discerned between good and evil. And they suppose that they have become perfect and blessed by their fathers. For those, my children, are like the birds which made their nests in the air and [yet] descended to the earth, so the hunters seized them through the deceptive tricks. And this befalls them because of their reliance on

---

213 Cf. Genesis 3:5.

themselves, and their working according to the desires of their hearts, and the fulfillment of their will, and their lack of obedience and not listening to their fathers. Then the devil brings upon them deceptive visions and fills their hearts with pride, in that he makes them see dreams at night and makes them come true in the day, to deceive them. And not only this, but also he brings them lights in the night, so that their dwelling becomes lit up. And he makes many such things and signs, which we cannot enumerate and write one by one. All these he does for them, so that he may reassure their hearts that he is an angel of God, so they receive him to themselves. And when they receive him as such, he drops them down quickly from their height—as we mentioned concerning those birds—because of the spirit of pride which seized them and made them think that they had become great and exalted in spirituality more than many others; therefore, they no longer listen to their fathers. And so what is written is fulfilled in them, "They are lustrous clusters that are bitter."[214] And they are so in truth, for learning from the fathers became hard on them, because of their thinking that they know everything.

7. Therefore, my blessed children, understand what I said to you, for you would not be able to progress and grow further, nor would you be perfected and know to discern between good and evil, unless you listen to the teaching of your perfect

---

214 Cf. Deuteronomy 32:32 LXX.

fathers. For so did our fathers do, by listening to their fathers and learning from them, and so they progressed and grew and became teachers, as it is written in the Wisdom of Joshua the son of Sirach, "Learn from your fathers, for they had learned from their fathers."[215]

So, my children, you ought to imitate those who obeyed their fathers and listened to them in everything. And their fathers taught them all the works of God, which they had learned from their fathers, and they became teachers to their believing, obedient children. For Isaac obeyed Abraham, Jacob obeyed Isaac, Joseph obeyed Jacob, Elisha obeyed Elijah, Paul obeyed Ananias, and Timothy obeyed Paul. These, and others like them of the saints, obeyed their fathers, and performed their will by being obedient[216] to them in everything, and knew the truth, and learned righteousness, and finally became worthy of the Spirit of God. Then they began uttering the truth in everything, as it is written, "I have made you a ruler for the house of Israel."[217]

So now, my beloved in the Lord, who are upright in their hearts, if you desire to advance and grow overmuch, and to become untroubled in your hearts, and for the demons to be unable to mock you in anything, then listen to your fathers and obey them—and you will not fall.

---
215 Cf. Wisdom of Sirach 8:9.
216 "Being obedient" is literally "fulfilling the obedience."
217 Cf. Ezekiel 3:17 LXX.

8. And I will teach you another work, which would confirm man from beginning to end: that he ought to love God with all his soul, and with all his heart, and with all his intent, and that he ought to offer Him worship. And then God grants him a great power and joy, and all the works of God will be sweet to him like honey. Also all the labors of the body, and the rumination, and the night vigils, and taking the yoke of the Lord, [all these] will be light [and] sweet for him.

For the sake of our Lord's love for men, He launches on man things contrary to these, so that he may not become exalted, but [rather] he may remain steadfast in the struggle, and may grow all the more; for[218] in place of power he receives heaviness and weakness, and sorrow in place of joy, and anxiety in place of rest and stillness, and bitterness in place of sweetness, and many such things suffers the one who loves God. But he is strengthened greatly in the struggle against them and overcomes them. And if he overcomes them, the Spirit of God will be with him in everything and will strengthen him, so that he is not afraid at all of any evil thing.

And I beseech my Master, that He may give you this grace for the sake of your obedience and may preserve it for you. This is He to whom, with His Father and His Holy Spirit, is due praise and sanctification from all rational [beings], forever. Amen.

---

218 This appears in *The Paradise of the Spirits*. *Expanded Paradise*: lest.

THE TWELFTH LETTER

To his children, the monks, informing them that against those who have reached perfection and have received the Holy Spirit, fiercer warfare must be launched than the first [ones], so that grace may be confirmed for them, and that they may increase in their perfection and receive the last blessing.

1. Know, my beloved children in the Lord, that the Holy Spirit is from everlasting, eternal, who gives a sweet-smelling aroma that cannot be described by a tongue. As it is said, "Who are they who knew the delight of the Spirit and His sweetness, except those who were worthy that He dwells in them?" And this is known, that many are not worthy of Him, because the spirit of repentance does not abide in the souls of the repentant except after very many labors. So, if it [i.e. the spirit of repentance] abides in her [i.e. the soul], it entrusts her to the Holy Spirit, and the

Holy Spirit dwells in her.

We might see, my children, that in this world there are things that resemble this. That is, precious stones are not acquired except through much labor, and are not found in cities and villages, but in kings' houses only. Likewise, the Holy Spirit also does not abide in a haughty soul, but in the souls of the humble, whose thoughts are all on perfection. Therefore, if this Spirit abides in these, they offer to the Lord great thanksgiving and much glorification, for they were worthy of the dwelling of the Holy Spirit in them, as Levi became worthy and offered to the Lord great thanksgiving, saying, "I bless You, O Lord, You who have taught me by the Spirit, whom You gave to Your servants," and as he also said, "Blessed are You, O Lord, for You have given honor to Your saints, better than all riches, and I cannot comprehend the greatness of the richness of the Spirit, whom You bestowed upon Your saints."

2. And this Spirit, my children, [whom] the saints sought and found, is the true Stone, which was mentioned in the Holy Scripture: "A merchant seeking beautiful pearls, who, when he had found one pearl of great price, went and sold all that he had and bought it."[219] It is also written that [He is like a] "treasure hidden in a field, which a man found and hid; and for joy over it he goes and sells all that he

---

219 Matthew 13:45–46.

has and buys that field."[220] My beloved, likewise are the saints, in all generations; when they found this Spirit, and He dwelled in them, they offered great thanksgiving to the Lord. For He does not dwell except in the souls of such blessed [people], and reveals to them great mysteries, and gives them joy and rest for their hearts in this world, and makes their night like the day.

My children, having made known to you some of the works of the Holy Spirit, I would like to make known to you also the battles of the evil spirit. Therefore, know that since [the time] that I parted from you, the Lord facilitated my way until I reached my dwelling, and I was confirmed in my solitude, outside the community, through the assistance of the Holy Spirit, secretly and manifestly. And I would like you to be always near me, so that I may make known to you what the Holy Spirit reveals to me at all times, for it is written, "The riches of the Lord help the wise," and what are the temptations which befell my poverty after that. For the temptations, in truth, do not come with [such] power except upon those who received the Holy Spirit. For at their receiving the Spirit, temptations come upon them from the devil, because the Spirit releases him against them. For the devil has no authority to force any of the believers [to obey him], unless he is given this from the Holy Spirit.

---

220   Matthew 13:44.

3. And our Lord Jesus Christ, when He took what is ours, became an example for us, so that He may teach us always that we [ought to] know the truth. For when He was baptized, the Holy Spirit came upon Him like a dove. Then the Holy Spirit drove Him into the wilderness to be tempted by Satan. When he tempted Him with all temptations, he did not prevail against Him, as was said in the Gospel of St. Luke, "Now when the devil had ended every temptation, he departed from Him until an opportune time. Then Jesus returned in the power of the Spirit to Galilee."[221] And likewise are all those who receive the Spirit and struggle and overcome the temptations, for the Holy Spirit strengthens them, and gives them an exceedingly great power, and lifts them up, and preserves them from all things.

My beloved children, I desired that you were near me, to know my last temptation, which resembles the last temptation of our Lord Jesus Christ. For when He completed His economy and knew of His departure, He said, "O My Father, if it is possible, let this cup pass from Me; nevertheless, not as I will, but as You will."[222] And this was through prayers and supplications, and it is not [out of] despair, or fear, or weakness[223], but [rather it is] for our teaching, also as His first temptations were for our teaching. For of His own will, He came down from heaven,

---

221 Luke 4:13–14.
222 Matthew 26:39.
223 Literally: inability.

in that He may not leave us, and dwelled upon the earth, and took our form to save us through it, by what He did in it of these works[224] and teachings. And He died for us, and was buried and arose, and saved those imprisoned in Hades, and ascended into the heavens where He was at first.

4. See then, my children, the love of God the Word, that He lifted us from the abyss of Hades to the highest heavens. For the heaven on high is other than the visible heaven; and the visible heaven is other than the atmosphere which is the air that blows through its lightness; and the air atmosphere is other than this dense earth, on which we presently exist and [yet] we will soon move away from. And know that the heavenly works are other than the earthly works, and that there is another region heavier than this dense earth, very hard and dark, and it has no light at all nor rest; and it is called Hades.

For the temptation which came upon me lastly, my children, brought me nearly to Hades itself, because the enemies of good wanted to cast me into it by their use of much cunning, and my labor and struggle and hardship and disturbance were about this. But I, the poor one, thank my God and glorify Him, He whom I have served with all my heart since my youth until now. And I listen to Him, because He has not abandoned me but has supported me

---

224 Literally: dispensations.

and saved me from the darkness of the enemies, and He has restored me to my first dignity once again, as He saved Adam and his righteous children and restored them to their first estate. For it is written, "He ascended on high, He led captivity captive, and gave gifts to men."[225]

5. And I make known to you, that my last temptation resembles Joseph's last temptation. For the blessed [and] righteous Joseph, when he was tempted with many temptations, was not troubled, and at last, when he was thrown into prison, which is a type of Hades, he was troubled by this temptation. But our Lord, through His compassion, when He saw the goodness of his struggle and his patience, gave him great honor and made him a king. And from that time on, he was basically no longer tempted.

For truly, my beloved children, I have not concealed from you the measure of the temptation I was in, from which my Master saved me. And I am certain that this was through your prayers, your supplications, and your remembrance of my poverty. Because you have labored exceedingly with me, the Lord will give you the grace of the Spirit and salvation, as He gave to my poverty. For He said to His disciples, "You are those who have endured with Me in My trials. And I prepare for you a kingdom, just as My Father promised, that you may

---

225 Ephesians 4:8; cf. Psalms 67:19.

eat and drink at My table in My kingdom."[226] And understand, my children, the sense of these words, that the one who partakes with the Master Christ in his obedience to Him, partakes with Him in the places of rest; and the one who partakes with Him in being dishonored, partakes with Him in glory. For whoever accepts the hardships, insults, reproaches, and dishonor, is he who is glorified. For it is written that the good son is the one who inherits the labors of his fathers and their blessing. As for the evil son, he inherits the curse.

6. And know, my beloved children, that after I wrote this letter, the Spirit moved me to write to you about the Seraphim [or the Cherubim], which Ezekiel the prophet saw, which are a type of the believers' souls who struggle and receive perfection. This had four wings, full of eyes, and had four faces looking to the four directions. One face was like the face of a man, the second the face of an ox, the third the face of a lion, the fourth the face of an eagle. As for the rest of what the prophet mentioned, this is not the [right] time for me to write about it. But I will explain a little to you on the interpretation of that, and if I come to you, through the Lord's help, I will explain to you the rest of it orally, because I cannot write to you about it.

Therefore, know that the first face of the seraphim, which is the face of a man, is a symbol

---

226 Cf. Luke 22:28–30.

for the believers who are in the world, who do the commandments belonging to them. If one of these goes out to [pursue] the form of monasticism, he is likened to the face of the ox, for he labors and is diligent in the commandments which belong to monasticism and the palpable warfare. If he completes [the duties of] the cenobium according to its order, and he goes out and lives in the wilderness and is set apart in solitude to wage war against the invisible demons, then he is likened to the face of the lion, who is the king of the beasts of the wilderness. So if he overcomes the invisible enemies and has dominion over the passions and reigns over them, then he rises through the Holy Spirit, beholds the divine visions, and is likened to the face of the eagle. And in him will be fulfilled that which is written, "Your youth is renewed like the eagle's."[227] His mind then discerns what comes to him from his six directions, so he is likened to the six wings [which are] full of eyes, and he becomes a spiritual seraph and inherits the eternal inheritance by his obedience to his spiritual fathers.

7. And I know, my children, that all of us have received power from the Lord because of our obedience to our fathers and their blessing for us. And you also, for your obedience and service, receive power from the Lord and inherit the blessing of your fathers. And truly I say to you, that I make mention of you always and behold you in the Spirit,

---

[227] Psalms 102:5 LXX, OSB.

like the tender, compassionate mother for her young children. Many times my Master desired to give me rest from the labors of this body, and to take my soul to Him. But, for the sake of the rest of the Lord's Spirit upon you, He left my poor spirit in her body, in order to rear you, and He said to me, "You are a good mother and a righteous nursemaid, and I have left you to rear your children well." And now, my blessed children, receive my last blessing.

8. Behold, your father's book and his blessing to you; therefore, keep it, because it is the true inheritance and legacy of the spiritual fathers [to their children]. For they give neither gold, silver, nor such things, as an inheritance to their children, but the true inheritance. As for the fathers according to the flesh, they give gold, silver, and things like these, as an inheritance to their children. Look to the patriarchs, how they were exceedingly rich in gold, silver, and the like of corporeal riches, and [yet] it was not mentioned that they saved anything of these to their children, because they are temporal, transient. Rather, they gave them the true blessing that lasts forever as inheritance, which gives the heavenly rest as an inheritance, and it remains with man forever.

And know that this blessing, which your father gave to you, is like the fatherly blessings, a salvation in the Lord. May our Lord give to you the Spirit of truth[228], until you depart from this transient world and inherit the everlasting one, through the intercession of all our saintly fathers. Amen.

---

228 *The Paradise of the Souls*: May the Spirit of truth give you guidance.

THE THIRTEENTH LETTER

His last letter, which he wrote to his beloved disciple Paphnutius, who was the head over his children the monks, to everyone under his obedience, and to all who seek the path of the Lord. He emphasizes that they ought to remain steadfast in their places, and not to move from them, that they may receive the last blessing. And in this [letter], he informs them about the kinds of the demons' wars and the kinds of the Lord's help, to those who endure.

1. My beloved in the Lord, the honorable Paphnutius, peace be to you.

Before all else, I pray for the sake of your salvation, and also for the sake of the salvation of all the souls who are obedient to you, who pray with you in the name of the Lord, and [for] all those who walk with you in peace, for the sake of our Lord

Jesus Christ.

The Lord Jesus Christ will give comfort in the kingdom of heaven to those who give comfort to their fathers' souls. And know, all of you, that whoever gives comfort to a single man of the servants of the Lord, even with a cup of cold water, his reward will not be lost, according to what our Lord said by His pure mouth, "And whoever gives one of these little ones only a cup of cold water in the name of a disciple, assuredly, I say to you, he shall by no means lose his reward."[229] He also said concerning those who grieve and offend the disciples by their evil: "But whoever causes one of these little ones who believe in Me to doubt, it would be better for him if a millstone were hung around his neck, and he were drowned in the depth of the sea."[230] And He also said, "With the measure you use, it will be measured back to you."[231]

Understand this, my beloved, that the Lord does not love anything of what is upon the earth more than His disciples and those who do His will, and He hates all who hold them in contempt. For whatever a man does to the servants of God, whether good or evil, he does to Him, because He said, "He who receives you receives Me,"[232] and He also said, "Inasmuch as you did not do it to one of the least of

---

229 Matthew 10:42.
230 Cf. Matthew 18:6.
231 Matthew 7:2.
232 Matthew 10:40.

these, you did not do it to Me."[233]

2. Therefore, my beloved, be on your guard against despising anyone of the people, for the root [of contempt] is pride, which brought[234] the anger of God upon the people of the world. Therefore, Isaiah the prophet said, "For the day of the Lord of hosts shall come upon all who are proud in their hearts and insolent."[235] So, my beloved, see the greatness of this sorrow which afflicts the proud. Therefore, we also ought to weep for ourselves in agony of heart and sorrow, for I have seen many monks and virgins who have fallen into this intractable[236] passion because of their corrupt opinion, for they say about themselves, "We are a great thing and there is no one like us." And truly, my beloved, I say to you that there is nothing in them but pride, contempt for people, hatred, evil jealousy, and strife. And they do not desire to repent and return with their hearts. And these and such like them have not made them discern between good and evil, and between sweetness and bitterness, for the malicious spirits in the air made them weep at the time of laughing, and laugh at the time of weeping, and the saying of the Scripture is fulfilled in them, "Cursed are all who make good evil, and evil good, and who make the

---

233 Matthew 25:45.
234 Literally: necessitated.
235 Cf. Isaiah 2:12 LXX.
236 Or: difficult.

bitter sweet, and the sweet bitter."[237]

For those ought to have heard the saying of St. John: "Do not trust every spirit, but test the spirits, whether they are of God."[238] But we ought to weep for those who are confirmed in the aforementioned evils all the days of their lives, these which they love more than their necessary food. And they do not hear the true teaching of God, but hold onto these evil teachings which are of the spirits of malice.

3. And these are the teachings of God: purity, continuous peace that is without change, which is full of mercy, and the rest of the good, true fruits, whose perfection is the blessing. Therefore, my beloved, strive to acquire these teachings which are of the Spirit, through which our souls shall live and we shall receive the Lord in ourselves, because they are the safe path, in which there is no thief or anything evil.

And know that, without purity of body and heart, no one can be perfect before God. As it is written in the Holy Scripture, "Blessed are those whose hearts are pure, for they shall see God."[239] Perfection, then, is born of purity of heart, for there are two kinds in the heart: I mean, the natural good, and unnatural evil which gives rise to the passions of the soul—that is, slander, envy, mocking, and the

---

237 Cf. Isaiah 5:20 LXX.
238 Cf. 1 John 4:1.
239 Cf. Matthew 5:8.

rest of the evils. As for that which is good, it gives rise to the knowledge of God and the salvation of the soul from these passions; therefore, David the prophet said, "Bless the Lord, O my soul ... who heals all your diseases."[240]

Therefore, my beloved, if a man strives, through lack of evil and [through] trusting in the Lord with uprightness, and flees from the evil things, through weeping, sorrow, sighing, fasting, vigilance, meekness, and many prayers to God, then the Lord, through His goodness, supports and saves him from all the passions of the soul. As David the prophet said, "Judge me, O Lord, for I have walked in humility, and I have trusted in the Lord; therefore, I shall not fear."[241]

4. And as I have made know to you, my beloved, that by these works the souls are healed of the passions, I also make known to you that many have lived all their lives in monasticism and virginity, and [yet] they have not learned the pure teaching, because they have left their fathers' teaching and held onto their hearts' desires. Therefore, the malicious demons and the mutinous thieves that are in the air prevailed against them, and began hurling arrows at them secretly night and day, so that they may make them not remain steadfastly in their cenobia, kindling their hearts with pride, vainglory,

---

240 Psalms 102:2–3 LXX, OSB.
241 Cf. Psalms 25:1 LXX.

evil jealousy, slander, anger, fury, obstinacy, and many other passions. These and such like them the demons make, because they intend our death, not our life.

This word which I teach you, my beloved, is not my own, but James the Apostle mentions it, saying, "But if you have bitter envy and discord in your hearts, do not boast and lie against the truth. This wisdom does not descend from above, but is earthly, sensual, demonic."[242] It is also written in the epistle of John the Apostle, "He who sins is of the devil."[243]

Now that you have learned, my beloved, that the Lord does not work in those established in these deeds. Rather they are participants of the demonic teachings and are counted with the demons. Therefore, let us weep for ourselves at this time of sorrow which we are in, and let us also know the measure of [the greatness of] the gift of the Holy Spirit, crying out with the one who said, "Come, let us worship and fall down before Him, and let us weep before the Lord who made us."[244] And let us also recite his saying, "Save me, O Lord, for the holy man has ceased; the truth has diminished from among the sons of men. Each one speaks to his neighbor with deceptive lips and a double heart."[245] And because of these words and what follows after

---

242 Cf. James 3:14–15.
243 1 John 3:8.
244 Psalms 94:6 LXX, OSB.
245 Cf. Psalms 11:2–3 LXX.

them, it is right for us to weep, for he said, "The Lord destroys the deceptive lips and boastful tongues."[246]

5. And know, my beloved, that these are they who are counted with the five foolish virgins, for they have passed all their life in foolishness. And they have not bridled their tongues and have not purified their eyes and bodies from the lusts, nor [have they purified] their hearts from uncleanness and many other things, because of which we ought to weep,[247] for they are impure. They were satisfied by the mere wearing of wool, which is the garb of virginity, and no more. Therefore, they did not have the heavenly delight, and did not mourn over themselves, and did not light their lamps. Therefore, the bridegroom does not open to them, but he says to them as he said to the foolish virgins, "Assuredly, I say to you, I do not know you."[248] And he also says to them, "Depart from Me, you cursed, into the everlasting fire, where there is weeping and gnashing of teeth."[249]

6. And now, my beloved, I have not written this letter to you, except because I seek the salvation of your souls, that you may be free, and faithful, and a pure bride to Christ. For He is the Bridegroom of all the pure souls, as Paul the Apostle says, "For

---

246 Cf. Psalms 11:4 LXX.
247 This clause is literally: which deserve that we weep because of them.
248 Matthew 25:12.
249 See Matthew 25:41 and Matthew 13:50.

The Thirteenth Letter

I have betrothed you to one husband, that I may offer you as a chaste virgin to Christ."[250] And I know that many wars have befallen you, my beloved, and through the help of our Lord, who guided you[251], you have passed them one after another, for God is true, and He is the one who strengthens you and strengthens all who serve Him, "who will not allow you to be tempted beyond what you are able."[252]

Then know, my children, the power of the trials which befell you, and the greatness of the honors which God granted you because of them. And remain steadfast in what will come upon you also, for gold is tried in the fire many times, so that it may appear chosen, through the much trial. Likewise our Lord, through His goodness, tries man with many trials, and through them He molds him, like the refined gold, and He teaches him the warfare of the heart, so that he no longer thinks or mentions the insults and dishonors which men inflicted upon him. And he will also be without fear of the deeds of the devil, but he humbles himself before God and trusts in Him, and he is always ready, through what is good, before God, as David the prophet said, "My heart is ready, O God, my heart is ready; I will sing and give praise in my glory."[253]

7. And know that this [following thing] must

---

250 Cf. 2 Corinthians 11:2.
251 That is, who managed your affairs.
252 1 Corinthians 10:13.
253 Psalms 107:2 LXX, OSB.

happen to you: that some of your brethren would make you sorrowful, by insults and reproaches, but [even] that your companions in your dwellings would debase you. Therefore, if this befalls you, be immovable, and do not fear nor be sorrowful, but thank the Lord for all these. For without Him, you would have had none of these, for wars must come against the servants of God. And whoever is not tested, through the goodness of God, by trials, sorrows, hardships, and tribulations, so that he may learn how to acquire patience and what is good, he will not receive honor from God.

Therefore, now, my beloved, endure the hardships and sorrows which come upon you, and thank the Lord in great humility, that you may see the gladness of your labors, and may rejoice like Susanna the strong in war, who prevailed against the lust of the two law-breaking elders who bore false witness against her and imposed on her many hardships. And through her patience and steadfastness, God lifted her up at the end of her struggle, and He humiliated her enemies. And you may also rejoice like Thecla the strong in spirit. For she was not afraid of her parents' insults against her; neither was she afraid of the fire also, nor of the one who was in charge of torturing her, nor of the ferocious beasts. Finally, the Lord granted her gladness of heart and the rewards of her labors. For the power of her faith in God quenched the fires, and shut the mouths of the ferocious lions, and humiliated all her enemies.

[And you may rejoice] like Joseph also, who was humble before God and men. For when his brothers envied him, hated him, and wanted to shed his blood out of [their] great envy, because they saw that he was honored by their father, divine providence guarded him from being killed. But they exercised authority through jealousy, and lifted up their hands against him, and finally sold him as a slave. Then the wife of his master, to whom he became a servant, caused him many hardships, to the extent that he was thrown into prison. And he was chaste, meek, very pure, without spot, [in both] soul and body. Through the Lord's help, he was not afraid of all these straits, but he was patient and trusted in the Lord. And finally, God lifted him up and made him ruler over Egypt and all its districts. As for his brothers who envied him, the Lord humiliated all of them under his feet!

8. My beloved, those whom I mentioned, and [others] who ran their course, did not receive honor from God at the start of their struggle and their trials, but after He tested them and molded them with tribulations and hardships, He made them know how to face the combats. Then when He saw that they were patient in the tribulations and hardships, and that they made the Lord their hope, He gave them the honor of His Divinity, and He humiliated under their feet those who hated them. My beloved, when I bring to mind the struggle of

those and their reward, my spirit rejoices with joy and gladness, and I pray for your sakes imploringly. Therefore, stand fast through patience, and let not your hearts become weak in your tribulations, but thank God for them, so that you may receive from Him the reward for them.

9. I have written these letters to you, my brethren, and to all who are called in the name of the Lord, so that all of you may have peace, truth, and the love of God, and your love for one another, and so that there may not be among you quarrelling, slander, evil thoughts, worry, resistance, hostility, evil jealousy, lack of obedience, pride, reviling men, mocking them, debauchery, love of vainglory, hatred, desire for beautiful garments for the body, nor enmity against one another. And behold, my poverty implores you, that you do not let any of these works [or qualities] be in yourselves nor among you in the place where you dwell. For the anger of the Lord comes upon the cenobium wherein such works are [present].

10. And know, my brethren, that our lives[254] in this world are very short; therefore, take heed in them, be diligent, and do not squander [them], lest your departure from it comes while you are harboring hatred toward each other, and so you are counted with the murderers, according to what is written,

---

254 Literally: ages.

"Whoever hates his brother is a murderer."[255] These sayings and commandments are not for monks and virgins alone, but are for all the believers who share, with them, in the catholic, apostolic Church of the Lord Christ.

And now, my brethren, let each one of you forgive his companion, that the Lord may forgive you. For the Holy Scripture urges us to this, by saying, "Forgive, and you will be forgiven."[256] And if anyone of you is wronged, let him accept this with joy, and surrender the matter to the Lord, for He is the just Judge who recompenses. And the one who has wronged his companion, let him hasten and humble himself before the Lord, and plead with his companion that the Lord may forgive him. And my beloved, do not let the sun go down on your wrath, as the Scripture teaches us,[257] but take away from your hearts all the evil thoughts which you concern yourselves with, or which you think against each other, so that the enmity may be dissolved, whose root is hatred and envy. For these two passions are very evil, and are despised by God and men, and ought not to be present in any believer or servant of God. Therefore, my beloved, if these matters were present among you in the past, from now on be careful that they are not present with you, and do not let them have authority over you.

---

255 1 John 3:15.
256 Luke 6:37.
257 Ephesians 4:26.

11. And know that the days of our life are very few. But in them we can return to the Lord from our sins, lest our departure, from here to there, overtake us unawares; and we cannot then return here, for we see that those who have departed do not return to us. We also do not wait for their return, but await going after them. And this is inevitable upon all the people of the world, from beginning to end.

For this [reason], my beloved, none of us ought to boast about the abundance of his foolishness, and say, "I have prevailed against my companion, and I have no compassion upon him." Let the one who said this word, or who was thinking it, know that he has given power to death over himself only, so his portion will be in the place of weeping and the gnashing of teeth and the worms that do not sleep and the fire that is not quenched. Having known this, my beloved, let us struggle as long as we are in this body, and treat the wounds of our souls, before our time has come to an end. And let these sayings be constantly in our minds, that we may do them before our souls leave our bodies, because our Lord, the just Judge, will send His servants, and they will seize the soul and will separate it from this clay house. At that time, all those who are found negligent regarding their salvation will be kept in the uttermost darkness until that fearful Day. And the bitter judgment will be issued against them, and they will be delivered to the merciless torturers and heartless jailers, placed on guard of that fire which is full of the worms that do not sleep, and of the outer darkness and the treasuries full of coldness and bitter cold. And these cruel [ones], to whom those will be delivered, will cast them into these places which are far from God, so that they may take vengeance upon them.

Then they will be full of weeping, crying, lamentation, and wailing, and no one will hear them or be merciful to them. For mercy has gone far from them forever, because they showed little mercy in their lives. For they did not feed the hungry, did not give water to the thirsty, and did not offer shelter to the stranger; the naked they did not clothe, the sick they did not visit, and to the one in prison they did not go. Therefore, their recompense was without mercy. They were also full of sin, deceit, and disobedience to the disciplining teachers and fathers, and they did not repent, not even for one day, and they did not take for themselves a teacher who prays for their sakes, and they did not give thanks for the abundant riches they were given. They also abandoned the knowledge of the Lord here, and He too will not know them there, but He will deliver them to those who have little mercy, that they may take vengeance upon them in the places of torment which are never ending; like the servant who showed no mercy on his companion in servitude and did not forgive him the hundred denarii which are paltry in comparison to the thousands which were forgiven him,[258] and like the powerless, lazy servant who buried his master's silver,[259] and like the one who had no wedding garment on,[260] and like the servant who rejects his master's commandment, and [who began] eating, drinking with the drunkards, and having no compassion on his fellow servants.[261] All those will be delivered to torment and to the people who have little mercy, for they were merciless, according to what is written, "For judgment is without mercy to the one who has shown no mercy."[262]

12. My beloved, because of my great compassion on you, I again implore you, I the poor one, that we ought to come to our senses[263] as long as we are in this body, and weep for ourselves, and sigh with all our hearts night and day, so that we may be delivered from bitter torment, weeping, sighing, and the sorrow which never passes away. Let us not lie down nor walk in the wide gate and the broad way which leads to destruction, and there are many who walk in it. But let us enter by the narrow gate and the difficult way, which causes sorrow, which leads to life, and there are few who enter by it. Those who enter it are the truthful laborers, who receive the rewards of their labors with joy, who inherit the

---

258 See Matthew 18:23–34.
259 Matthew 25:18.
260 Matthew 22:12–13.
261 Matthew 24:49.
262 James 2:13.
263 Or: awake.

kingdom.

So, the one who has made ready, my beloved, ought not to slack off from [going to] the harvest, lest the season ends, and then the one who wants to buy finds no seller. For this is what befell the five foolish virgins when they did not find anyone to buy from, and then they cried out and wept, saying, "'Lord, open to us!' But he answered and said, 'Assuredly, I say to you, I do not know you.'"[264] This did not befall them except because of their laziness, for if the Lord of the house arose and shut the door, then nothing would be of benefit, as was written.

And I will give you another example for this. When Noah entered the ship, him, his sons, his sons' wives, and the rest of [those] who were with him, the Lord shut the door of the ship because of the flood water which came upon the evil-doers. And Noah did not open the door of the ship. Neither did he permit his sons to look at that fearful scene which was a condemnation of those [who were] evil. Nor did those evil-[doers] come, after the door was shut, to board [the ship] with the righteous. Therefore, they became of the goats on the left, where they cannot draw near to those who are on the right. And so they perished by the flood water, because of their laziness and disobedience. For Noah, in the hundred years in which he built the ship, warned them, [yet] they did not obey him nor hear him. So

---

264 Matthew 25:11–12.

they perished.

13. So now, my beloved children, who care about [having] peace with everyone, I beseech you, through God's grace, that you hear me; and then I will also hear you. And let us all hear the Lord who said on the prophet's tongue: "Who is the man who desires life, and loves many days, that he may see good? Let him keep his tongue from evil, and his lips from speaking deceit. Let him depart from evil and do good; Let him seek peace and pursue it,"[265] and the rest of the saying. This is my gladness, I and the brethren who are with me, that we hear of your Christianity, and that the peace of the Lord may be with you and among you, and that you build upon it every day and night, so that you may become one spirit with one will, one faith, one fellowship, one table, that peace may continue for you.

And since [the time] your letter has reached me and until now, I have had sorrow of heart because of trouble that happened among you, because of the lack of discernment of the one who wants to set himself apart alone and to do his own will, while he is [living] in your midst. From now, my beloved, let this not be [so] among you, but fulfill [that is, partake of] the bread of the house of peace in concord, for it is not necessary that his bread is given to another place. Rather gather together in one spirit, and fulfill it in peace, concord, humility,

---

265 Cf. Psalms 33:12–14 LXX.

the fear of God, and prayers. And then the bread of the house of peace is fulfilled, and you receive it with joy and gladness. Afterwards, you give to the weak and poor, so that you may be worthy of the second, elect joy, which is faith, hope, love, humility, fear [of God], discernment, asceticism, peace, rumination, and the love of the brethren. For whoever has these is wearing the wedding garment[266] and is walking in the commandments of the Spirit.

14. Truly I say to you, my beloved, that until now the Lord has not given me [permission] to do this matter, that is, my separation from the brethren. And I am afraid of doing it of myself alone, without the Lord's will. And I ask you to remain steadfast in your places[267] and your patience, that these sufferings may pass away from you, for this is not the [right] time for you to ask for this matter. And whoever has progressed and reached [the measure] for this to be his, I know that our Lord will make him known to me and will fulfill His good will. If you remain steadfast on this, then you will have peace, and your places, and whoever comes to them, and whoever prays in them in the name of the Lord.

And know this with certainty: whoever strives according to the will of God, with which the will of man is not mixed, will be then supported and strengthened by the power of God, which is sweeter

---

266 See Matthew 22:12.
267 *The Paradise of the Souls*: humility.

than honey and is full of all gladness. And it will give marvelous works to his soul, and will prepare before him all the ways the Lord loves. Then none of the enemies can oppose him, for they see him walking in the will of the Lord. As for the one who strives according to his own will, supposing it to be the will of the Lord, God will not support him in anything but will leave him to the demons, that they may dwell in his heart night and day. And they will not allow him to have any rest at all, for his heart has become darkened, not seeing any light at all. They also will make him powerless in all his affairs, the manifest and hidden, because of the absence of grace, and they will inflict him with many other things, hard and toilsome, which I cannot utter. Many have gone astray because of that, for their lack of understanding and discernment, and they began mocking the believers who were walking well in the midst of the cenobium.

15. And this is what happened to our first father, because he had little discernment and listened to Eve. For Eve went astray through having little discernment, and she coveted immortality and deification when the devil, hiding his form in a serpent, spoke to her as one who had love for her, saying, "If you ate of this tree, you would be gods and would not die."[268] Through having little discretion and her lack of discernment, when she heard about

---

268 See Genesis 3:4–5.

deification[269] and immortality, she did not test the one speaking with her, that she may know that it is the devil, but she cast away from her the will of the Lord, and she broke His commandment. And thus she acted presumptuously and made Adam act presumptuously, and both fell, after the sublime dignity, into this worsening disgrace, for they disobeyed the will of the Lord.

My beloved, likewise in truth everyone suffers who casts away from himself the will of the Lord, and who does the will of his heart. And so the saying of the wise Solomon, in the Proverbs, is fulfilled in him, "There is a road that seems to be right, but its end reaches into the depth of Hades."[270] And I make known to you also that the devil gives such as those joy and gladness, which are not so in truth, but [they are] frowning, sorrow, and weeping, because they are not from God. For the joy and gladness that are from God are rather given to those who labor with all their strength, do violence to themselves[271], and force themselves to remain steadfast in good works, and who cut off their wills and hold onto the Lord's will.

And having spoken about the will of the Lord and the will of men, I desire to make known to you another thing; that is, the will which works in the heart of man is of three kinds. Many monks and

---

269 Or: the matter of the Divinity.

270 Cf. Proverbs 14:12 LXX.

271 Or: compel themselves.

virgins do not consider this, but very few of them, who have labored in mighty struggles and have become perfect through discernment, these observe this. For it is written, "Solid food belongs to those who are strong."[272] The first kind [of the wills] is from the devil, the second is from man, and the last is from the Lord. The two which are from the devil and man, with them God is not pleased, but He is pleased only with the one which is from Him.

16. And now, my beloved brethren, who are beloved of my heart, examine yourselves, and hold onto the will of God, and listen to your father. For I pray abundantly to God for your sakes. And do not leave your dwellings with the excuse of goodness, which is not goodness, and move to another. Rather, remain steadfast until I come to you through the Lord's help, and I will make know to you what is to your benefit. Because if you did this matter, you would make my heart sorrowful, and you would be sorrowful yourselves too. And I, the poor one, my beloved, think that I possess the knowledge of God's will more than you do, and that I know what is [good] for your correction. Therefore, remain steadfast in the love of the brethren and in the glory that is yours, and consider[273] the will of the Lord. This is not a contemptible thing, that a man always considers [that is, observe] the will of God in everything. And truly I say to you, that if a

---
272 Cf. Hebrews 5:14.
273 Or: contemplate.

man does not abandon all the desires of his heart, and [if he does not] humble himself in everything, and [if he does not] cast away from himself all his wealth and possessions, and [if he does not] listen to the Lord through his listening [that is, through his obedience] to his spiritual fathers[274]—he cannot consider[275] the will of God, nor can he do it. And he will be deprived of the last blessing.

17. For when Abraham blessed Isaac, he said to him, "My God strengthen you, that you may do His will." And likewise everyone who obeys his spiritual fathers in everything, does the will of God. And also our righteous father Jacob, who was blessed by his father Isaac for his great obedience to his parents, in him the powers [that is, the virtues] dwelled, for he used to listen to them and do their will. Concerning him it was mentioned in the Pentateuch[276] that before the death of his father and after he received the blessing from him, his mother asked him to go to Mesopotamia and remain with his uncle Laban, because his brother Esau wanted to kill him. And Jacob did not desire to go there and leave his father's house, for he loved them and they also loved him. But he listened, obeyed, and went to that far place and to a land he did not know. He did not break the will of his mother, but he abandoned his desire

---

274 *The Paradise of the Souls*: listen to the Lord and to his spiritual fathers.

275 Or: contemplate.

276 Or: Torah.

and will, so that he may comfort her heart. And he strove [with] all this diligence until the blessing of his fathers was perfected on him, for it is written, "The blessing of the fathers establishes the houses of the children."[277]

And it has reached me that some of you say that Jacob did not flee from his brother Esau, and some others say that he fled from him. Both of these sayings are correct concerning him, for he did not flee by his will but fled by his obedience. Therefore, the Lord supported him in everything, hidden and manifest. Now, my beloved, let the remembrance of Jacob and those who followed his course, be with you and in yourselves unceasingly.

18. Eliminate from your minds what I have heard about you, for you say that God forgets your labors and does not reward you for them. Certainly not! For our Lord—glory be to Him—did not say that the reward would be here [on earth], but trials, tribulations, hardships, and sorrows, and the reward will be there. For this life is the way of hardships and trials. Therefore, if you endure, listen to, and obey your fathers, the Lord will do good in rewarding you, for this is the labor which is remembered before the Lord.

And I your father, the poor one, make known to you, my beloved, that I have labored in the mountains and deserts, and have prayed night and

---

277 Cf. Wisdom of Sirach 3:9 LXX, OSB.

day that the Lord would reveal His will to me. He revealed nothing to me, until I listened to my fathers in everything and received its knowledge from them [that is, the knowledge of the will of the Lord]. For everyone who listens to his fathers listens to the Lord, and the one who listens to the Lord listens to his fathers, and the one who does not listen to his fathers is not heard by the Lord. Therefore, my beloved in the Lord, listen to your father in what I have written to you, that his blessing my come upon you, and that you may find rest and grace and power and glory, and that the Lord may facilitate all your ways. Behold, I have made known to you in this letter, by my ways, the bodily and spiritual works, and the oppositions[278] of the body and of the demons, so that you may know and be diligent and receive the last blessing, and that a great grace may dwell in you.

And peace be to you all, and the salvation from the Lord Jesus Christ be to your humble spirits and to your purified thoughts and hearts. Let His blessing come upon every place where there is humility. To whom be the praise and glory and honor from all rational [beings], and to His Father and to His Holy Spirit, now and forever and ever. Amen.

---

278 *The Paradise of the Souls*: elements.

www.ingramcontent.com/pod-product-compliance
Lightning Source LLC
Chambersburg PA
CBHW051807040426
42446CB00007B/559